TRI-STATE REFLECTIONS

Tennessee, Alabama, Georgia

A small historical compilation
of people, places, and events
in Tennessee, Alabama and Georgia

Jerry H. Summers

Waldenhouse Publishers, Inc.
Walden, Tennessee

Tri-State Trivia Reflections: A compilation of short articles about persons, places and events in Tennessee, Alabama, and Georgia.

Copyright 2021.© Jerry H. Summers 1941. All rights reserved. No part of this book may be reproduced in any form or by any electronic or mechanical means including information storage and retrieval systems, without permission in writing from the publisher. The only exception is by a reviewer, who may quote short excerpts in a review.

Published by Waldenhouse Publishers, Inc.
100 Clegg Street, Signal Mountain, Tennessee 37377 USA
423-886-2721 www.waldenhouse.com
Printed in the United States of America
Editing, Type and Design by Karen Paul Stone
ISBN: 978-1-947589-45-2
Library of Congress Control Number: 2021947366

Seventy-six short stories illustrated by seventeen photographs and compiled by lawyer-historian, Jerry Summers, about lesser known but interesting persons, places and events in Tennessee, Alabama, and Georgia in the southeastern United States of America.

HIS036120 HISTORY/United States/State & local/South
HIS036060 HISTORY/United States/20th Century
HIS054000 HISTORY/Social History

Proceeds from the sale of **Tri-State Reflections** will go to Orange Grove Center (OGC), a 501(c)(3) Charitable organization under the Internal Revenue Status. Copies of **Tri-State Reflections** can be purchased directly from Orange Grove Center, 615 Derby Street, Chattanooga, Tennessee 37404 – or – www.orangegrovecenter.org.

Dedication

To the memory of Thomas Caldwell
One of the founders of Orange Grove Center in 1953
and who for sixty-five years served as supporter and unpaid legal counsel to protect the legal rights of the clients of the Center.

To the staff, teachers, parents, volunteers, and Board of Directors who have tirelessly given their time and support on behalf of the clients at Orange Grove Center.

Table of Contents

Preface ... 9
Foreword ... 11
Acknowledgments ... 12
Introduction ... 13

Tennessee Articles

Johnny Cash – Chattanooga City Limits Sign ... 15
The Popes of Pikeville ... 20
Shufflin' Phil Douglas ... 23
A Big Man – Willis Lawrence Taylor ... 27
John and Jane Clemens – Mark Twain's Parents ... 29
Mickey Mantle's McCallie Teammate- Sammy Joyce ... 32
Cas Walker – When Elvis Died ... 35
Judge Charles Galbreath – *Hustler* Reader ... 37
How Did Bookie Turner Get Acquitted ... 42
They Eliminated the Judge's Court ... 45
Herman Brown Killian - Politician ... 48
Election Day Practices in Chattanooga ... 52
Chattanooga City Elections – "Rolling the Vote" ... 54
Jitney Cabs in Chattanooga ... 56
Wine of Cardui – Wine for Women ... 59
Spring City Train-Bus Accident ... 63
Snake Handling in Tennessee ... 66
Chattanooga's – Negro League Nines ... 69
Glenwood Manor – Educational Academy ... 72
Middle Tennessee Mule Day ... 75
Hales Bar Ghost Inhabited Site ... 77
Pine Breeze's Sanatorium ... 80

The Suck 83
Ghosts of Sewanee 85
Lincoln Park – Vital African American Landmark 88
Brushy Mountain Penitentiary – Alcatraz Tennessee 91
Dolly Parton and the Greased Pole 95

Alabama Articles

Mentone Springs Hotel 97
Stevenson Railroad Depot Museum 99
Fort Payne, Alabama 102
Noccalula Falls Park 105
Russell Cave National Monument 108
Lost Towns of Alabama 111
Hotel Tutwiler - Birmingham 114
Coon Dog Cemetery 116
John Heisman – Football Innovator 119
Helen Keller – A Complex Life 122
Pat Trammell – Scottsboro & Bama's All American 126
David McCampbell – Alabama Air Ace 129
Howell Heflin – Justice and Senator 132
Big Jim Folsom – Alabama's Unique Governor No.1 135
Big Jim Folsom -No. 2 137
Big Ruby of Alabama 139
Fightin' Shorty Price & George Wallace 141
Phenix City – Original Sin City 144
John M. Patterson – Alabama Governor 147
James Edwin Horton, Jr. – Bravest Judge in Legal History 149
Worst Judge Over Scottsboro Boys Trial – William Callahan 152
Thomas E. Knight – Scottsboro Prosecutor 155
Chattanoogans at Scottsboro Boys' Trials 158
Drano Murder Case, A Lawyer's Price –Robert B. French, Jr. 164

Georgia Articles

"Doc" Anderson – Rossville's Psychic	167
When Dolly and George came to Ringgold	170
Judge Murphy Clagett "Red" Townsend	172
Howard Finster – Paradise Garden	175
Oliver Hardy – Harlem's Comedian	179
Jackson C. Pharris – Georgia's Pearl Harbor Hero	182
Before Marjorie there was Larry	186
Johnny Cash Meets Walker County Sheriff Ralph Jones	188
Who Were the Georgia Wool Hat Boys?	192
Susan Hayward's Georgia Connection	194
Leo Frank – Atlanta's Murder Victim	197
Rube Garland – Atlanta Advocate	200
Were the Wright Brothers First? – Micajah Clark Dyer	203
Ben Epps – Father of Aviation	207
Peerless Woolen Mills, Rossville, Georgia	210
Peerless Millers Baseball History	214
Peerless Clipper WWII Aircraft – Captain Lawrence Sies	215
Old Stone Church Museum – Ringgold, Georgia	217
Walker County's Fantastic Pit	220
Durham Georgia Coal Mines	222
Erosion of McLemore Cove	224
Walker County Courthouse War	227
Daisy's Ties to Last Georgia Legal Hanging	231
Beaten by a Bite – Gene Talmadge	234
Lula Lake Murder	236
Conclusion	239
History Sources in Our Area	239
About the Author	241

Illustrations

Johnny Cash Chattanooga City Limit Sign	16
Shufflin' Phil Douglas	26
Mickey Mantle	33
Wine of Cardui	61
Pine Breeze postcard and photograph	81
End of the Line Tennessee Moonshine	93
Stevenson Railroad Depot Museum	101
Noccalula Falls	105
Coon Dog Cemetery	117
Helen Keller	123
Pat Trammell	127
David McCampbell	130
James Edwin Horton, Jr.	151
Howard Finster - Paradise Garden	177
Water tower in Harlem, Georgia, featuring Oliver Hardy	179
Patent drawing of Micajah Clark Dyer's flying machine	205
Fantastic Pit, Walker Co. Georgia	221
Lula Lake Falls	238

Preface

Over the past few years of writing history articles for the *Chattanooga Times Free Press* and *Chattanoogan.com* I have accumulated over 300 published and unpublished stories about people, places, and events in local communities in Tennessee, Alabama, and Georgia.

My 2020 book, *Tennessee Trivia No. 1.* is a compilation of stories dealing only with the Volunteer state. Due to the proximity of Tennessee to its neighboring states of Alabama and Georgia, new avenues of topics provide an additional treasure trove of subjects in the three jurisdictions. Hopefully, these tales will educate the young and jog the memories of adults as we revisit events in the Tri-State.

The proceeds of all sales of both books will go to Orange Grove Center, 615 Derby Street, Chattanooga, Tennessee 37404 (423) 629-1451 as a tax-deductible charitable contribution under their 501 (c)(3) charter with the Internal Revenue Service.

Books can be purchased directly from Orange Grove Center for $22.00 plus $4.50 for shipping costs, or the shipping expense can be avoided by picking up the book at Orange Grove Center. Perhaps the book would be a good birthday present or "stocking stuffer" during the holiday seasons?

Foreword

The Southern states of Tennessee, Alabama, and Georgia have had many unique persons, places, and events during the years. Those described herein are just a small sampling of the interesting history of each state.

It is hoped that revisiting these incidents and individuals will not only awaken a new interest in the matters described, but also will stimulate further inquiry into the aspects of these three Southern states.

--Jerry H. Summers
2021

Acknowledgments

I would be remiss if I did not once again acknowledge the support that I have received from my well-qualified staff of attorneys who have allowed me to substantially slow down my involvement in the everyday practice of law while I engage in my writing activities.

Jeff Rufolo, Jimmy Rodgers, Marya Schalk and Ben McGowan have capably assumed the role of advocates for the individuals who have entrusted our firm to handle their legal cases.

Without their expertise and cooperation, I would not be able to continue researching and writing the articles contained herein on what is now my seventh book.

The willingness of John Wilson, creator, and owner of the website newspaper, *Chattanoogan.com,* to allow me to submit short historical articles to be published each Monday and Thursday is greatly appreciated.

The typing talents of our firm's receptionist, Joy Hayes, and her ability to decipher and correct the many mistakes in the rough drafts has always been appreciated.

Introduction

Several years ago, I started writing infrequent articles in the *Chattanooga Times Free-Press* on local historical events in the Perspective Section under Editor Chris Vass and with local writer and financial advisor Mickey Robbins. I subsequently starting writing two columns a week in John Wilson's website newspaper *Chattanoogan.com* under the Happenings Column and broadened the schedule of topics to include the sister states of Alabama and Georgia. These columns deal with the topics of persons, places, and things in those states as well as the Volunteer State of Tennessee.

The histories of the three states include many famous individuals, places, and events. In this publication, I have tried to accumulate stories about lesser-known persons and happenings that add colorful stories to some of those personalities and events.

This book is a compilation of only a small number of writings covering a variety of topics as the interesting list of subjects began to mushroom. If there is a sufficient interest in the contents, I hope to do other volumes that will also include more Tennessee, Alabama, and Georgia topics.

More importantly, the proceeds from the sale of the books will benefits one of my favorite charities, Orange Grove Center.

TENNESSEE ARTICLES

JOHNNY CASH – CHATTANOOGA CITY LIMITS SIGN

The life and legend of country music icon Johnny Cash have been memorialized through the media. His continuous battle to fight alcohol and drug addiction, his often unhappy first marriage and his "Ring of Fire" romance with June Carter Cash are part of his persona. His frequent reliance on religion and backsliding were just a part of his troubled existence. The "Man in Black" image of the Folsom and San Quentin prison concerts endeared him with many fallen individuals, and his albums were all top chart winners.

Perhaps the greater remembrance of his life is the concert in 1980 in Nassau Coliseum with Willie Nelson, Waylon Jennings, and Chris Kristofferson under the title of "The Highwaymen." This amazing display of the ability of great musicians to enjoy themselves and to equally share the spotlight to entertain their fans can frequently be seen on the Public Broadcasting Station on WTCI in Chattanooga as part of one of their fundraising programs.

Johnny Cash wrote and sang on many award winning albums that are an integral part of country music history. Album No. 66 by Cash entitled *The Baron* was released by Columbia Records in 1981. The title track was a top ten hit, and four singles were released with moderate success. All reached within the top 71 records but none were ever ranked higher.

The album cover showed Cash in a pool hall in his customary black outfit holding a pool cue. Cash always personalized his life's experiences, both good and bad. He also wrote on many subjects involving his home State of Tennessee and other surrounding areas. *Chattanooga City Limit Sign* is one of those songs.

After the song was written, Chattanooga City Commissioner of Public Works, Paul Clark, presented the singer with a replica of the sign which is present at the entry points to the Scenic City.

The album was recorded in March, 1981 at the CBS Studio in Nashville, Tennessee, with famed country music producer Billy Sherrill and included Janie Fricke and the Jordanaires as backup vocals. The song did not attain the longtime fame of *The Chattanooga Choo Choo*, but it did point out a humorous moment in Johnny Cash's struggle with his addictions, whether it was true or not.

On January 11, 2011, the song was sung on You Tube with the following lyrics:

Johnny Cash, left, receives a replica of the signs which mark the Chattanooga city limits from Chattanooga City Commissioner of Public Works, Paul Clark, right.

Chattanooga City Limit Sign

I was thumbin' a ride one Saturday mornin'
Outta Nashville totin' my sack
I lent my car to a gal that lived in Chattanooga
And she hadn't never brought it back
She was drinkin' pretty heavy when I let her have it
I hope she knows it was only a loan
Ain't no tellin' what I might have told her back at the time
But that ole car was also my home

About five miles out I was getting' kinda tired
Sweatin' hard and feelin' kinda weak
I woke up with no cigarettes and nothin' to drink
And I hadn't had a bite to eat
My nerves was so quick I couldn't tell where I was shakin'
Then a set of brakes sang my song
Some fella stuck his head out a '57 Chevy
And hollered hey man come on

I told 'em I was headin' down to Chattanooga
They said hop in we're going there too
And the way they took off in a cloud of smoke
I still ain't believin' it was true
They had their windows down and I was sittin' in the back
With my tongue still hung in my throat
He was hittin' just about a hundred and ten
And he said man what do you think of this boat

Well there was two semi's a strugglin' up ahead
One tryin' to pass the other
They had the whole road blocked so he passed 'em on the right
And let me tell you somethin' brother
I was so nervous that my teeth was clickin'
There wadn't no way my head could think
Then the one that was sittin' on the passenger side
Turned and said, Hey man you want somethin' to drink?

I just shook my head cause I couldn't talk
He said okay and then he said cheers
Them fools was drinkin' whiskey and wine
And then chasin' it down with beer
Well I started sweatin' that ol' sticky sweat
And I know I was white as a sheep
Then one turned the radio on wide open
And said, Hey man check that beat

By the time we reached the top of Monteagle
I thought I heard a rumblin' sound
And then I saw a sign that said fallin' rock
And right there I was floorboard bound
I was rollin' and squirmin' on the ol' floorboard
Too weak to sit or stand
And then the driver said we're doin' a hundred and twenty
Look here man no hands

I got up enough nerve to raise up and look
And by now there couldn't be no surprise
But his hair was blowin' all over my face
And dandruff blowed in both eyes
He never did drive on the right or left
He just kept on ridin' that line
I rubbed my eyes and saw the prettiest thing
The Chattanooga city limit sign

He slowed down and I said
Mister please I'd like to get off right here
He said aw ride on into town with us
We're gonna go down and pick up more beer
I said please once more and he stopped the car
And then he handed me my sack
Said they'd look for me on the road later on
In case I wanted to catch a ride back

I got out and sat down by the side of the road
Feelin' sick and lookin' mighty pale
I don't remember anything much after that
But next mornin' I woke up in jail
I didn't know anybody in my cell
And didn't wanna ask why was there
But they all kept grinnin' and turnin' their heads
And it was more than my head could bear

So I called the jailer and I asked him to tell me
Why I was there if he'd be so kind
He said for stoppin' the traffic
While I was huggin' and kissin'
The Chattanooga city limit sign

THE POPES OF PIKEVILLE

There have been many outstanding pioneer families in the Sequatchie Valley running from Pikeville in northern Bledsoe County through the adjoining counties of Sequatchie and Marion to South Pittsburg and the old town of Orme near the Alabama state line. One of the most prominent clans has been the Popes of Pikeville.

Jonathan Pope first came to Pikeville around 1802 after being born in 1786. Any genealogical chart of the history of Pikeville has been filled with Pope descendants. Without attempting to slight any member of the family limited space necessitates that we jump to the limb on the family tree to Lewis Shepherd Pope, one of the most widely known of the generations of Popes.

Lewis S. Pope was born on August 16, 1878, in the Sequatchie Valley near Pikeville. After attending both public schools in Pikeville and Peoples College he graduated from Emory and Henry in Emory, Virginia, and Vanderbilt Law School in 1900. In 1912 he was elected to the Tennessee Senate and serving in the 58th General Assembly and in 1913 he was appointed assistant district attorney for the Eastern District of Tennessee.

One alleged story in Lewis Popes colorful past was that in 1924 he was asked to represent Lem Motlow of the Jack Daniel's family in Lynchburg on a murder charge in St. Louis, Missouri. In 1910 Tennessee had voted "dry" on a statewide referendum and therefore the manufacturing of the renowned Tennessee sour mash whiskey was banned. As a result, Motlow had moved the company's distillery to St. Louis.

In 1924 Motlow, while intoxicated, had shot and killed a white conductor on a passenger train in Missouri. Lem claimed self-defense and the only eye witness was a black porter. He beat the murder rap through a crudely racist and high-priced defense strategy. Although he allegedly was broke because of the on-coming depression, Motlow tried to unsuccessfully hire Lewis Pope as his defense attorney by allegedly promising to pay him with stock in the liquor business which was virtually worthless at that time. Pope might have later regretted the rejection of the stock in the Jack Daniels Distillery.

Lewis would later run for governor of Tennessee in 1928 and 1932 as a Democrat. In 1928 he ran a poor third in the Democratic Primary but in 1932 lost to Henry Hill McAllister by only 9,000 votes. He claimed voter fraud by E.H. (Boss) Crump of Memphis and McAllister and chose to unsuccessfully run as an independent in the General election, finishing third again. He was an active trial lawyer and served as both a special prosecutor and defense lawyer in many of the sensational murder cases held in Bledsoe County which was reported by the late historian, Thomas K. Swafford in his three volume historical treatise on the Tollett-Swafford feuds and Bloody Bledsoe. Severity, frequency and violence exceeded the more famous Hatfield-McCoy conflicts in Kentucky and West Virginia.

In addition to the practice of law he served as a member of the Board of Directors at the First National Bank of Pikeville and served in many community capacities prior to his death on May 14, 1972. He also served in the cabinet of Governor Austin Peay. In fact, he served in the administration of five Tennessee governors.

Other Lewis Pope descendants include the Warden of the Tennessee prison system, Joe Pope and J. William Pope, Sr., who worked for Esso in the oil business for many years. Lewis Pope was the great uncle of J. William Pope, Jr., (February 2, 1938-June 8, 2014) who was an attorney, mayor of Pikeville, state legislator (1966-1968) and lobbyist in the Tennessee General Assembly for the short line railroads and unsuccessful candidate for Congress in the Third Congressional District of Tennessee in 1968.

In 1970 he was appointed District Attorney General by Governor Buford Ellington for the 18th Judicial District. He was known as a tough but fair prosecutor who engaged in many sensational trials in his district. He was not content to manage his office from afar but engaged in courtroom battles on a daily basis prior to his retirement in 1992. He returned to private practice in Chattanooga and served as a lobbyist in the Tennessee General Assembly prior to his death in June, 2014, from cancer.

The legacy of the Pope family as lawyers is being carried on by Bill's son, J. William (Jimmy) Pope, III, who is an assistant district attorney in the Rhea County office in Dayton.

The Pope family is part of the interesting, colorful, and violent history of the Sequatchie Valley from 1861 to 1950.

SHUFFLIN' PHIL DOUGLAS
(1890-1952)

The adjoining states of Tennessee, Alabama and Georgia have a connecting bond to a major league baseball pitcher from 1912-1922.

Phil Brooks Douglas was born on July 17, 1890 in Cedartown, Georgia, but moved to Cowan, Tennessee, in Franklin County where he grew up. He would also move to Birmingham, Alabama during his life. At 6'3" and weighing 190 pounds, Phil was a big man for that era. He began his professional baseball career in 1910 at the age of 20.

His fastball pitch was impressive enough that he would be favorably compared to future Hall-of-Famer Walter "Big Train" Johnson, often considered the greatest right-handed pitcher of all time.

However, their careers took distinctly divergent paths over the years. Johnson's major league career extended over twenty-one years, and he played for only one team – Washington, Senators.

Phil Douglas was a virtual vagabond and would be signed and released by five teams because of his alcoholism and tendency to disappear from his teams for days at a time. He would eventually be banned from baseball for life in 1922.

Phil's first season in organized baseball started in 1911 with the Rome, Georgia, team in the Southeastern League until it folded in July. That started an odyssey that included numerous minor leagues and the five major league stints.

Phil Douglas obviously had more than just size and a big fastball. Prior to it being outlawed, the "spitter" was the pitch that Phil and many other hurlers used as their dominant pitch, although he also would effectively rely on a curve, fastball, and change up. He learned his devastating spitball from Hall-of-Fame pitcher Ed Walsh of the Chicago White Sox. He was fined numerous times for violating training rules.

Douglas came from "a hard drinking Southern family and had developed a taste for alcohol as a teenager." He also had a love for fishing, and the two pastimes occupied much of his time on days off between pitching starts.

What would follow is a tragic story of a promising but unfulfilled career.

Alcohol and his inability to control this weakness was also aggravated by inconsideration by others including the acid and venomous tongue of John McGraw, the legendary manager of the New York Giants who had differences with many known players over the years.

Douglas did not have a Hall of Fame career, as he only had a record of 94 wins – 93 losses, but he had a career Earned Run Average (ERA) of 2.80 runs per game, which to baseball fans is excellent and in fact was tenth (10th) amongst National League pitchers over those nine seasons that Douglas played in the majors.

A twenty-one-page summary of his life by Mike Lynch can be obtained by Googling Phil Brooks Douglas. The work goes into great detail about the ups and downs of the talented performer on the baseball diamond who could not control the off-field alcohol demons.

Some of the events of his turbulent life are humorous, most are sad, and are indicative of a career which might have been but was not.

Babe Ruth of the New York Yankees once described Douglas, "As tough a man as I've seen [in the American League]," and even John McGraw called his performance, "Among the best pitching that has ever been displayed in a World Series."

However, Douglas' slide to the bottom continued amidst tales of his alcohol binges and unsubstantiated allegations that he might have thrown or offered to throw ball games to get revenge against McGraw and the New York Giants finally led to Commissioner Kennesaw Mountain Landis banning him from baseball for life in 1922.

Landis had been working to crack down on crooked players in the wake of the infamous 1919 Black Sox scandal where several players had accepted money from gamblers to lose games where they were heavy favorites against the mediocre Cincinnati Reds.

Banned from his lifelong profession, Douglas would wander from one semi-pro team to another accepting nominal pay for limited appearances. In 1925 he pitched in Pikeville, Tennessee; Tracy City, Tennessee; Lynch, Kentucky; Bluefield, West Virginia, and at times when not drinking, displayed some of his potential greatness. At the age of 38 he would pitch regularly for the local Cowan team, and he often beat squads from Tennessee and Alabama.

After his first wife died in 1927, his descent into the liquor bottle started over. It did not subside until he remarried in 1928 and lived in several Tennessee towns in Tullahoma, Nashville, Whitwell and Bon Air.

After his career was over Phil became a foreman for a state highway crew in Jasper, Tennessee, until 1949. Injured on the job, he would reside in poverty in a log cabin in Sequatchie, Tennessee, living on his meager state pension.

After suffering three strokes he died on August 1, 1952 at the age of 62 and is buried at Tracy City, Tennessee.

To the end of his life, he maintained he was innocent of the charges that led to his ban from baseball, but each request by friends to Commissioner Fay Vincent to be reinstated both during and after his death were denied.

In 1979, author Tom Clark wrote a book on the life of Douglas titled, *One Last Round for the Shuffler* (Pomerica Press) which emphasizes the failure of the player to use his natural talents to achieve greatness. It is still available at several publishers for prices ranging from cost of a used paper back for $6.50 upwards to $100 for a hard cover, depending on condition.

He would earn his nickname because of the slow pace with which he "shuffled" from the bullpen to the mound.

Phil Douglas would be described in an 1938 article as one of the "outlaw" ball players for their often-outrageous conduct on and off the playing field. These included Hall of Fame caliber players such as Shoeless Joe Jackson, Buck Weaver, Hal Chase, Eddie Cicotte and Douglas.

Phil Brooks Douglas was a unique individual who had lifelong ties to the Sequatchie Valley and Cumberland Plateau in Tennessee.

Shufflin' Phil Brooks Douglas

A BIG MAN – WILLIS LAWRENCE TAYLOR

On August 6, 2010, a big man in stature and reputation passed after a long battle with kidney disease at the age of 69. Nobody knew him at the University of the South (Sewanee) by the name above but if you mentioned "Will" everyone who attended the school on the Cumberland Plateau between the late 1950s and 2003 would remember him with affection.

Born on January 11, 1941, in Winchester, Tennessee he began working as a cook in the Gailor dining hall as a teenager. To the young men who waited on tables, Will was always full of fun and life.

He would work for Aramark Food Service at Sewanee until 2003 when he had to retire because of kidney disease that required him to be on dialysis for several years. He would finally pass in his sleep of a heart attack related to his prior illness.

He met his future wife, Delores, who lived in Lynchburg, Tennessee, while she was visiting in Winchester. After they married she also was employed at Sewanee, and in 2020 after 38 years, Delores is the Building Services Manager in charge of forty-three custodians, two supervisors, and two furniture movers at the University.

Will was also a popular bartender during the party weekends when the consumption of alcoholic beverages rules were less rigidly enforced than the present.

Will was always a popular spectator and fixture at Homecoming and football weekends on Hardee Field. Alumni that returned to the Mountain after several years and who belonged to the old Waiters Guild would receive a big smile and hug from Will if they ran into each other at the games.

Will and Delores had three children, Brian, Willis, Jr. and Eric. He loved them equally, but his interest in football was intensified when his son Eric, after graduating from Franklin County High School, and Memphis State University, was drafted as a defensive tackle by the Pittsburg Steelers in the 7th round of the 2004 National Football League

(NFL) Draft. Subsequently Eric would play for the Minnesota Vikings, Seattle Seahawks and Tennessee Titans.

In the Canadian Football League, Eric would play for the Edmonton Eskimos, Toronto Argonauts, British Columbia Lions, and Calgary Stampeders before retiring as a player and returning to Franklin County High as an assistant football coach and teacher. His dad died on August 6, 2010, and a lot of fond memories of "Will" still survive to this day amongst students who worked with him.

His funeral services were conducted in All Saints Chapel at Sewanee and interment was in Watson-North Memorial Park in Winchester.

JOHN AND JANE CLEMENS – MARK TWAIN'S PARENTS

Was Mark Twain conceived in Tennessee?

Much is known about the life of the famous humorist and author Samuel L. Clemens, aka Mark Twain, but his parents John and Jane Lampton Clemens were the biological parents of five children born in Jamestown, Fentress County, Tennessee.

Their sixth son, who is recognized as one of America's greatest icons and whose career included also being a printer and journalist, a steamboat pilot, a gold-silver miner, a newspaper editor, author and publisher, was born on November 30, 1935 in Florida, Missouri.

John Marshall Clemens (1798-1847) was a lawyer, and he and his bride of one year, Jane, settled in the town of Jamestown, Tennessee. In 1825 their first son, Orion, was born. By 1827 the family had moved to Jamestown, and in addition to producing more children, John became active in the development of the community and was elected circuit clerk of the court.

Twain's father had come from a prominent Virginia family that owned both land and slaves in the Commonwealth. He subsequently moved to Columbia, Kentucky, and at the age of 21 became a licensed attorney.

On May 6, 1823, the family moved to Fentress County, and in addition to practicing law and serving as court clerk, John operated a general store and also was a county commissioner and acting attorney general.

From 1832-1835 John was the postmaster in Pall Mall, Tennessee, and also was an unsuccessful land spectator. He built the local jail and courthouse.

Sometime in the spring of 1835 the family moved to Florida, Missouri, where their famous son would be born on November 30, 1835. According to some authorities John and Jane Clemens were still residing in Frentess County only five months and twelve days prior to the birth of their sixth child, Samuel Langhorne Clemens (Mark Twain).

Thus brings up the issue that has divided the American public both prior and subsequent to the United Supreme court decision of Roe v. Wade (1973) dealing with the subject of abortion as to whether a person's age be determined from the moment of conception. If you are an anti-abortion advocate, then it becomes obvious that Mark Twain's mortal existence began in Jamestown, Tennessee.

When the family moved to Missouri in the spring of 1835 they took with them Jamie, the house girl and slave, along with then five children and leaving behind 75,000-100,000 acres of land.

In Jamestown there is a Mark Twain American Legion Post 137, a Mark Twain Park, and there is a ten room boutique hotel named after him. It is owned and operated by Sharon Garrett, the gracious widow of lawyer Skidmore Garrett, at 104 S. Main Street at the corner of Highway 127 and Highway 52 on the town square. (931)879-5475.

John Clemens erroneously believed that with his wealth in property he had secured a rich future for his many children. However, this assumption proved to be false, and in spite of leading a grandiose life style the anticipated great wealth faded away.

John in the meantime built an elaborate and elegant residence and played the role of an aristocrat wearing expensive clothes in the rural community. His wife dressed in calico dresses while their neighbors wives' dresses were homespun.

After several unsuccessful ventures and suffering from ill health, John accepted a promising invitation to move to Florida, Missouri, from John A. Quarles, the husband of his wife's sister, Patsy. John Quarles offered his in-laws a partnership in his store and encouraged John Clemens to renew his practice of law which he had previously left in Tennessee.

They later moved to Hannibal, Missouri, in 1839, but Clemens' business ventures continued to be unsuccessful. He was active in civil matters and would become a county judge and steamboat and railroad commissioner. John died in March of 1847 from pleurisy and pneumonia.

The Clemens had five sons and two daughters. Hypothetically the following question has to be asked. If the State of Missouri should concede that Mark Twain was born a citizen of Tennessee, could his bust or statute be allowed to be placed in the Tennessee Capitol in light of his family and his personal background dealing with slavery and under the present day movement to eradicate history and the memory of anyone who had anything to do with that subject?

Perhaps Tom Sawyer and Huckleberry Finn will be next to be abolished from the literary world?

MICKEY MANTLE'S McCALLIE TEAMMATE (ARNOLD "SAMMY" JOYCE)

One of the McCallie School's all-time athletic greats was also a roommate of Hall of Fame member of the New York Yankees, Mickey Mantle.

Sammy Joyce was also the original emcee for the musical group "Found Sam and the Dismembered Tennesseans" which evolved into the legendary "Dismembered Tennesseans" under the leadership of the late Frank McDonald and the late Fletcher Bright. Other members of the group were Lorrie Runge, Ansley Moses, John Baker and Bob Dickerson. Fletcher Bright quipped about Sammy, "He was a great guy, but he couldn't sing a lick."

When Sammy graduated from McCallie he played two seasons in minor league baseball and then served in the Air Force. He was replaced as emcee of the musical group by Frank McDonald of the *Chattanooga News Free Press* family.

"Sammy" Joyce was a letterman in football, basketball, and baseball at McCallie and was the recipient of the Stephen Athletic Medal as a junior and honoree of the Billy Wemyss Trophy for the Best Spirit in Athletics his senior year.

He signed a minor league baseball contract with the New York Yankees in 1948, and in 1949 he was assigned to pitch for the Independence Yankees in the Kansas-Oklahoma-Missouri League, a Class D minor league.

Mickey Mantle was on the team as a 20 year old outfielder. Although Sammy only played in 32 games and Mickey in 37, they developed a lifetime friendship. They allegedly roomed together during that short season and found time to have a good time as part of a fun-loving group of players at Independence, Missouri.

Bus trips with water pistol duels were a common occurrence that included watermelon fights in hotels they stayed in while on the road.

Innocent walkers outside the hotel would often be deluged with plastic bags filled with water from above.

Sammy developed a heart condition, and in 1991 a dinner was held in his honor at the Town and Country Restaurant by a group of friends. Mickey Mantle did not forget his former teammate and was in attendance. Also in attendance with Mickey was another Hall of Fame member, Enos "Country" Slaughter, Irv Noren of the Washington Senators, and another minor league teammate, Bob Wiesler.

Mickey Mantle

Sammy continued to be in baseball after his playing career was over. He was a scout for the Chicago Cubs and was involved in the club signing of Meigs County star athlete Ronnie Campbell as a third baseman. Unfortunately, Ronnie wound up behind future Hall of Fame member Ron Santo and never got to play beyond Triple A ball, but he did play at that level for 7 seasons. He did have a brief appearance with the Cubs.

After Sammy and his wife, Teresa, got married and had a son, Sammy, he remained active in coaching young baseball players in youth leagues including the Dizzy Dean League for 13-14 year olds. His teams won many championships, and his efforts to help youngsters were not stopped by heart attacks or strokes.

Around 1963 he formed a baseball team, "Thompson Twins", to play in the amateur Bi-State League. He built a team mixed with former minor league players, college players and other skilled amateur players. The roster included former Memphis Chicks catcher, Arnold Davis, former San Francisco Grants farm team member, Finley Bandy from Dayton, and former Chattanooga Lookouts outfielder Dan Porter.

Recent City High graduate Bill Eiselstein started at shortstop but was signed by the Atlanta Braves to play minor league baseball. He left the team to play two seasons with their farm club.

After Sammy's death in 1997, Fletcher Bright and a group of his friends and the McCallie School established a substantial scholarship in his name to help a deserving young athlete who needs financial assistance to attend the prestigious school next to Missionary Ridge.

CAS WALKER – WHEN ELVIS DIED

Only Knoxville's Cas Walker, entrepreneur, could come up with a scheme to make a profit out of the death of Elvis Presley, the King of Rock N' Roll. As stated in his *Cas Walker, My Life History*, the master grocery promoter from Knoxville, Tennessee, displayed his marketing genius in spite of having a limited education.

Upon learning of the death of Elvis, Cas sent an employee to Memphis to be at the Shelby County Courthouse at 8:00 a.m. when it opened. She was instructed to tell the Deputy Clerk in the Probate Division that she was a reporter from the *Watchdog* newspaper and that she wanted to purchase a copy of Elvis' will which had already been filed for Probate. Since Elvis had died its contents became a public record and available for purchase. (The *Watchdog* was Cas' newspaper that he distributed free to his customers. It was a forerunner to *The National Inquirer* that was based on sensational facts and sometimes rumors.)

Cas' agent was able to purchase five or ten copies of the will and then went immediately to the funeral home where Elvis' body was being prepared for transfer to Graceland. The enterprising employee represented that she was Elvis' niece and convinced the funeral home staff that she should get to ride in the limousine to the late singer's home. Supposedly, "They let her ride over, let her open the casket, and let her set the casket like she wanted for people to look at."

She took the cover off Elvis' face and took a picture of him in the casket. The picture of Elvis was on the front page of the *Watchdog* that week. According to Cas, he reproduced 10,000 copies of the will and sold them for $1.00 apiece with every $10.00 grocery order. All were sold out that week, so he had another 10,000 copies to be distributed at his out-of-town stores in Virginia and North Carolina. After those 10,000 were sold, Cas had more printed to take to Georgia and South Carolina and sold them to an individual for $1.50 each. Finally Cas sold additional copies for $2.00 with a $20.00 grocery order.

Cas proudly claimed that it was one of the biggest deals that he had done and was "one of his greatest promotional ideas"! Although he would get sued for libel a few times for outrageous things he printed, no lawsuit was ever filed about the Elvis will caper.

The *Watch Dog* would eventually go out of business when a police officer got a large judgment in a libel suit. Bizarre as it may seem, it was a great idea and promotion by Cas Walker.

JUDGE CHARLES GALBREATH – *HUSTLER* READER (1925-2013)

The public normally perceives the images of judges to be solemn wearers of black robes who, in an often stern manner, make decisions that affect the rights of citizens on issues of law and order and civil justice.

Occasionally, there will come along a renegade judicial officer who does things in a different way. Such was Charles "Charlie" Galbreath. When he died in 2013 at the age of 88, he had served the citizens of the State of Tennessee as a member of the Tennessee Court of Criminal Appeals, state legislature and often defender of the downtrodden and helpless.

He was also considered to be one of the most outspoken and flamboyant members of the judiciary in the State of Tennessee. Charlie's first ambition was to be an actor in legitimate theatre before the started his controversial legal, political and judicial career. He was a Nashville native, and his father owned several grocery stores. In the 1940s he actually studied drama at Carnegie Hall in New York City prior to entering law school at Cumberland Law School in Lebanon, Tennessee.

His study of drama stayed with him as he began the practice of law, and his flamboyancy also stayed with him to the end of his career. The combination of stage and gavel "often led to the chagrin of colleagues and opponents alike." Perhaps his most notable contribution to the legal profession was when, as a member of the Nashville Legislative delegation. In 1963, he spearheaded a bill that created the state's first public defender position in Nashville. He left the legislature to become Tennessee's first attorney to provide legal assistance to poor defendants who could not afford a private attorney.

As a result the public defender system was extended to all judicial districts in Tennessee's ninety-five counties. The *Nashville Tennessean* did a profile on Charlie in 1968 prior to his election to the Tennessee Court of Criminal Appeals which described him as a, "loved, elusive enigma." The paper further stated, "He has always made the legal profession a little nervous."

Following his election to the Court of Criminal Appeals, Judge Galbreath engaged in several unusual acts, such as performing marriages while he and the wedding couple were riding on a Ferris wheel. He also performed weddings in local bars in Nashville. Perhaps the most controversial action in conservative Tennessee was to write on court stationary a letter to his friend, Larry Flynt, editor of *Hustler Magazine* concerning the legality of such acts of sodomy that were considered "unnatural and illegal in some states."

Unfortunately, he did not use the legal terminology for such acts but described them using gutter language that shocked and upset Tennessee's legal establishment. The language would reverberate for years amongst Tennessee lawyers and probably formed the basis for the initiative for him to be cited by the Judicial Standards Commission in 1978 as the first judicial officer to be cited to a proceeding to "remove a judge from office."

The fact that his outspoken letter was on court stationery that contained the names of the other eight judges did not endear him to his colleagues. The Court of Criminal Appeals was created by the legislature in 1968 to hear trial court appeals in felony and misdemeanor cases as well as post-conviction petitions. The three judges sitting on panels in Knoxville, Nashville and Jackson rendered opinions which could be appealed to the Tennessee Supreme Court which exercised discretionary authority whether to grant the appeal.

Former Tennessee Bar Association President Landis Turner of Hohenwald has written about the *Hustler Magazine* letter. When the issue with Galbreath's article came out at the Tennessee Bar Association convention in Memphis, the purchase of the magazine at the Peabody Hotel's magazine stand, "Sold out of *Hustler* in less than an hour."

After liquor by the drink legislation was approved by voters of Davidson County, Charlie Galbreath and Landis Turner celebrated at the

Gaslight Lounge in Printers Alley in Nashville. Turner credited Judge Galbreath with, "Drinking bourbon on the rocks as the first drink and he (Turner) had a martini as the second."

Judge Galbreath was also involved in the Hamilton County case of contempt rendered against television host and wrestling promoter Harry Thornton had refused to identify the telephone caller who claimed he was on the grand jury investigating whether City Judge Bernie Harris had taken bribes from bail bondsmen and who claimed that the case was "whitewashed" by District Attorney Edward E. Davis.

After Thornton refused to name the caller, Criminal Court Judge Tillman Grant found him guilty of contempt and ordered him to be incarcerated in jail immediately. Recognizing that Thornton was probably going to jail, his young lawyer had prepared a writ of *habeas corpus* and had sent another young lawyer to Nashville to wait until Judge Grant ruled against Thornton. Then the lawyer was file it immediately.

Judge Galbreath, without granting the writ and with no notice to the State, set a hearing before the Tennessee Court of Criminal Appeals and released Thornton on his own recognizance. The State later appealed Galbreath's ruling to the Tennessee Supreme Court, which set the case for a hearing and set a bond of $1,000. Eventually the Supreme Court would accept the case and ruled that Galbreath lacked jurisdiction in the case and therefore could not release Thornton. Later the case was dismissed as being moot because the term of the grand jurors, and the grand juror who allegedly violated his oath of secrecy, had done so after the grand jury had gone out of session.

The Judicial Standards Commission identified several grounds for Judge Galbreath's removal from office.:

1. his 1976 letter on official court stationary printed in the *Hustler Magazine* discussing his preferred sex acts in vulgar colloquial terms;
2. his arrest in Columbus, Ohio in 1977 for jaywalking;
3. his 1977 press conference criticizing a "sting" conducted by the Nashville Police Department;
4. his decision to allow his law clerk to engage in part-time practice of law;

5. the manner in which he prepared opinions and worked with his colleagues on the Court of Criminal Appeals;
6. his derogatory public statements regarding the Commission, and
7. his alleged breach of a privately negotiated agreement to resign in return for the Commissions agreement to drop charges against him.

One uncharged incident was that he sold contraband Cuban cigars out of his law office. After the first hearing, the Commission recommended that Judge Galbreath be removed from office on all seven charges.

Upon receipt of the record and the Commission's recommendation, the Lieutenant Governor in the Senate and the Speaker of the House each appointed five legislators to a Special Joint Committee on Judicial Standards. The Committee determined that they would not consider three of the seven charges against the judge because they involved conduct that was not related to actions he had taken in his judicial capacity. The Special Committee had hearings from April 10-12, 1978 at which both sides presented witnesses.

At the conclusion of the hearings, the Special Commission determined that the judge's letter to *Hustler Magazine* was "inappropriate" although only three members of the ten-person Special Committee voted to remove him from office based on his *Hustler* article comments. The Special Committee found that other public comments by Judge Galbreath were either "improper" or "inappropriate" bud did not justify his removal from office. The Special Committee then formally reported back to the Lieutenant Governor and Speaker of the House.

The Senate took up the report on April 26, 1978. Following debate the Senate decided to vote on only two of the specific charges relied upon by the Judicial Standards Commission. By a vote of 18-4-1 the Senate decided that Judge Galbreath be removed based on his letter to *Hustler*. By a vote of 18-11-2 the Senate voted to remove Judge Galbreath from office by his characterization of members of the Judicial Standards Committee as "sons of bitches."

However, the results were four votes short of the number required to remove the judge from office because Article VI, Section 6 of the Constitution of Tennessee requires a super-majority of two-thirds of the members of each chamber (House and Senate). Ironically, the House of Representatives never voted on Judge Galbreath's removal.

On April 27, 1978, both legislative bodies separately passed resolutions assailing the Judge on the ground that his conduct, "Flouted the letter and spirit of the Code of Judicial Conduct." Shortly thereafter Judge Galbreath announced his resignation from the Court of Criminal Appeals and his intention to run for a seat in the General Assembly.

The colorful judge, always ready for a publicity stunt, held a "derobing" ceremony in the courtroom of the Supreme Court Building in Nashville. When he died in March 2013 from Alzheimer's disease and pneumonia at the age of 88, the legal profession lost one of the most colorful and controversial jurists.

HOW DID BOOKIE TURNER GET ACQUITTED! (1917-1986)

James E. (Bookie) Turner was a colorful and controversial law enforcement officer and politician in Hamilton County from 1958-1975.

He was one of eight children and was a student at Chattanooga Central High School. He was a Navy Veteran who served on the battleship USS Tennessee during World War II. His nickname "Bookie" allegedly came from his other siblings who claimed that although he professed a love of reading, he also used that as an excuse to get out of family chores.

Bookie was co-founder of Turner Funeral Home with two of his brothers. Eugene became a colorful and also controversial politician in his own right. In 1940 Bookie was appointed Hamilton County coroner and claimed to the youngest person to hold that position in the United States.

He defeated Republican V.W. "Red" Maddow in 1958 to become Sheriff of Hamilton County and served three two-year terms before being elected to the position of Fire and Police Commissioner for the City of Chattanooga in 1963. In 1971 he was defeated by former FBI agent, Gene Roberts, and lost his final race for mayor against Pat Rose in 1975.

He was re-elected as Commissioner for another term in 1967 while under indictment in federal court at Chattanooga for allegedly taking bribes for allowing the entry of moonshine whiskey into Chattanooga. According to the government, he was paid fifty cents per gallon for each quantity being delivered into the municipality without fear of criminal prosecution.

Turner was indicted for a conspiracy that included Gordon W. White, Sheriff E. Penney, George G. "Buddy" Hendricks and thirty-seven other unindicted (not charged) co-conspirators who were participants in the lucrative liquor scheme.

Bookie hired famed Watergate and successful Jimmy Hoffa prosecutor, James F. Neal of Nashville, to defend him. Co-counsel was the widely respected civil attorney, John K. Morgan of Chattanooga. The government was represented by two Department of Justice prosecutors from Washington, D.C. and local United States Attorney J.H. Reddy.

Because some of his three co-conspirators had lengthy criminal records and Turner had none, his lawyers tried unsuccessfully to get a separate trial from them on the grounds of unfair prejudice. Bookie had refused to make any public statement but, on several occasions, claimed that he, "Would tell his story when he took the stand."

The trial took over three weeks. The government presented a barrage of participants in the moonshine industry, including manufacturers, drivers, distributors and operators or purchasers of the illegal product that was sold in "good-time houses" and to private citizens and clubs.

The government, relying upon Bookie's repeated pronouncements that he would tell his story to the jury when he took the stand, made the fatal mistake of putting on just enough evidence to overcome a Motion for Judgment of Acquittal. At the end of the government case, it intended to get the case to the jury and was saving all of its strong evidence to cross-examine Turner when the he testified.

Senior District Judge Robert L. Taylor from Knoxville recessed the court until the next day and instructed the defense to meet and decide what would be their order of proof of witnesses. The defendants and their lawyers met as ordered, and what occurred has been substantiated by two independent sources.

This history is not intended to be a criticism of Bookie Turner's lawyers, James Neal and John Morgan. They had professionally attacked the government's case. A less talented old-time lawyer (Crawford Bean) suggested the strategy used, which had the effect of the government's being unable to further prove the case against Bookie by cross-examining him. The government was unable to put on what is known as "rebuttal proof" to contradict his testimony.

Juries acquit defendants for two reasons: 1. they believe the accused was not guilty; or 2. the prosecution fails to prove the guilt of the defendants "beyond a reasonable doubt" pursuant to the instruction given to the jury by the judge.

According to sources in the jury room discussions when the defendants and their lawyers met, Neal and Morgan asked each attorney if they were going to put their defendant on the witness stand. Crawford Bean, attorney for George G. "Buddy" Hendricks replied that his client was not going to testify because he had a criminal record.

Bean, after stating that his clients were not going to testify, shocked the group by saying that Turner would be a fool to testify because the prosecution had produced very little evidence against Neal and Morgan's client. He would be devastated and convicted on the evidence the prosecution was holding back to use on cross-examination of Bookie.

This statement produced a turmoil with Neal and Morgan stating that their client had to testify because of his "previous claims to exonerate himself from the witness stand."

After much discussion and attempted efforts by his lawyers to have him take the stand, Turner shocked the crowd and said, "I'm going with Crawford" (Advice not to testify).

Neal and Morgan, in order to protect themselves in the event Turner got convicted over their urging him to testify, had Bookie write out a document that stated that they had advised him to testify, and if he was convicted, that he had not taken their advice. This document has been lost in time.

Turner was acquitted and his co-conspirators were convicted. The reader can reach his own conclusion as to whether Bookie would or would not have been found "guilty" or "not guilty" if he had taken the stand to testify.

Neal and Morgan remained great lawyers throughout their illustrious careers. But for one case, an old timer like Crawford Bean better understood the thinking of the twelve jurors that decided James E. Bookie Turner's fate!

THEY ELIMINATED THE JUDGE'S COURT

One of the most unusual cases in the history of the judiciary in Tennessee was the Tennessee Supreme Court decision of Harold Duncan v. Rhea County, reported in 287 S.W.2d 26(1955).

Although the facts which led to the action of the Tennessee legislature's passing Chapter 570 of the Private Acts of 1953 are not stated in the above decision, they are relevant and important. Said private act was a simple repealing Act undertaking to revoke Chapter 868 of the Acts of 1949 which had established a Court of General Sessions for Rhea County, Tennessee, for an additional division in Spring City, Tennessee, north of Dayton.

Harold Duncan was a practicing attorney who was elected as the incumbent judge of the above division and after his court was eliminated by the 1953 Act of the Tennessee legislature, he filed suit asserting his right to continue and hold the office until his eight year term of office expired on September 1, 1958.

Judge Duncan had won his case in the lower trial court, and Rhea County had taken the extraordinary action of getting the Tennessee General Assembly to pass the 1953 act which simply did away with the Spring City Division of the General Sessions Court occupied by Judge Duncan. Duncan appealed on the grounds that the elimination of his court violated his rights under the Tennessee Constitution.

We will now fill in the facts omitted by Justice Swepston in his opinion upholding the elimination of Justice Duncan's Spring City division on December 9, 1955, and finalized in overruling a rehearing petition on February 3, 1956.

It appears that the sport of "cockfighting" was regularly engaged in by the citizens of Spring City in the northernmost municipality of Rhea County, although it was illegal under the laws of the State of Tennessee. The "sport" is defined as a blood sport in which two roosters specifically bred for aggression are placed beak to beak (pitted) in a small ring and encouraged to fight to the death.

Although illegal in all fifty states, the practice still persists across the nation and the "World Series of Cockfighting" is yearly held in Louisiana. Tennessee in the 1950s (and even today) was an active venue for such sport although opposed by the Humane Society of the United States.

On an undisclosed date and location in Rhea County sometime prior to 1955, a large crowd gathered to enjoy the gory slaughter of the doomed roosters in a circular cockpit. Frequently the contest's excitement was elevated by the consumption of the presence of both legal and illegal alcoholic beverages in additional to wagering on the outcome of the deadly contest.

Law enforcement had been informed of the scheduled event which was attended by a large crowd. Officers decided to conduct a raid, which upon their arrival, resulted in a wild scattering of the spectators fleeting the premises. Unfortunately for some, they did not all get away, and one of those arrested was the Honorable Harold Duncan, General Sessions Judge.

The cases came to be heard on Judge Duncan's docket, and he made the fateful decision of not recusing (declining to hear) himself from the cases of his colleagues and his own date with destiny. He listened attentively to the testimony of the law officers in all of the other defendants' cases and then made the judicious decision to dismiss all of their cases because of lack of evidence or because of illegal searches and seizures under the Tennessee constitution.

Having dismissed all of his co-defendants cases, he then proceeded to rule on the only remaining cause on the docket – his own. According to historical rumor his logic in dismissing his case was very simple.

"If the others weren't guilty how could he be guilty?"

Unfortunately, the Tennessee Supreme Court later held that it was proper to just eliminate Judge Duncan's court rather than address the facts and the provision of Article VI Section 7 of the Tennessee Constitution which holds that:

"Judges shall at stated times receive a compensation for their services to be ascertained by law, which shall not be increased or diminished during the time for which they are elected."

Simply stated, Rhea County could not fire Judge Duncan but they could do away with his Court! – (and they did!)

HERMAN BROWN KILLIAN - POLITICIAN?
(1921-2007)

If you asked anyone from South Pittsburg or Marion County in Tennessee if they, or any of their relatives, ever knew or heard of the above-named individual the answer would probably be "No!"

However, if you asked them if they were familiar with the name of "Yap" Killian, the recognition signals would immediately bring into play many interesting, colorful and often humorous stories of how things were done in the rural middle Tennessee areas during the period of his life from 1921-2007. The origin of Killian's nickname "Yap," as provided by one of his sons, is said to have been given to young Herman Brown at an early age due to his propensity to talk with a "gift of gab."

A second originator of the name "Yap" is alleged to be South Pittsburg native, Howard McReynolds, whose mother and sister would later become postmasters of the South Pittsburg post office. The fact that they were from Pikeville and relatives of Congressman Samuel McReynolds may have helped the two ladies get the political appointments.

Another family member of Yap claims that a friend used the term to describe him while they were in the military. "Yap" was a 1941 graduate of South Pittsburg where he was an outstanding athlete and remained an avid sports fan and golfer in his later years. He enlisted in the United States Army Air corps the day after Pearl Harbor Day and served for seven years. He would later preside as Commander of American Legion Post 62 in South Pittsburg.

A lifelong Democrat, he first began his many years of public service in 1954 when he was selected as one of the Justices of the Peace (J.P.) by the Marion County Quarterly Court that preceded the creation of the General Sessions Courts in Tennessee in 1960 by the state legislature.

Jasper, Tennessee, during this period of time bore the reputation of being the "World's Biggest Speed Trap" for its vigorous enforcement of the Speeding laws on the Dixie Highway (US 41) which ran through the downtown county seat of Marion County at Jasper.

During this era Constables and J.P.s were entitled to a fee for every traffic conviction that occurred within the county limits. If a speeder was stopped by local or state law enforcement, they would be brought to the Marion County jail and given the option of paying an immediate fine or having their case put over to the next court docket for a hearing. They would have to pay for a bail bond or remain in jail until the court date. Since most of the serious violators were from out of state or county, the choice of their decision to a pay a fine became obvious.

The speeders, upon securing the payment of their fine and court costs, were free to go. The Constables and J.P.S each got a fee, and the City of Jasper or Marion County got some court costs for administering justice.

Yap was one of the three J.P.s charged with protecting the citizens from speeders by representing the South Pittsburg section of the county. Francis "Nappy" Pryor, Sr. was the Jasper legal representative. J.P. "Stormy" Mears was appointed by the Marion County Commission as an alternate to relieve or assist Yap and Nappy if additional judicial authority was needed.

Business was so booming that the J.P.s were provided a room with a bed at the Marion County Jail in order that instant justice could be administered twenty-four hours a day, seven days a week by the rotating magistrates.

It was a system that survived over the years until some disgruntled young local citizens belonging to the Junior Chamber of Commerce (Jaycees) became alarmed at the community's reputation of being the "No. 1 Speed Trap in America" and put up billboards to warn travelers entering the county limits to slow down to avoid criminal prosecution.

Marion County also was known to have "cockfights" within its corporate limits in the rural area of Powells Crossroads outside of Whitwell and other locations. Yap's involvement as a J.P. in the a cockfighting event has been re-told with different versions by his two sons,

Mike Killian who previously served as Mayor of South Pittsburg, and Bill Killian who was the United States Attorney in the Eastern District of Tennessee under President Obama. Both were very young at the time of the cockfight incident, and the readers will have to decipher which account is correct.

Mike claims that his dad was at the rooster fighting contest in the company of another individual who ran when law enforcement officers raided the event. While they chased his buddy, Yap was able to slip away and headed back to the Marion County Jail to go on duty. When the large groups of defendants were brought in on school buses, Yap's fellow magistrate J.P. "Nappy" Pryor was amongst those arrested and was in line to be processed at the jail.

After listening diligently to the evidence, Yap dismissed his colleague's case and lightly fined the other attendees. He was never arrested and did not have to make a decision on his own case like the Spring City General Sessions judge did (See: They Eliminated the Judge's Court, page 45) that resulted in the elimination of his division of the Rhea County Sessions Court.

Brother Bill Killian has a slightly different version of the cockfight incident. He claims his father was not at that particular event but was on duty at the jail when the non-supporters of the local Humane Society were brought in mass to the jail to have their fates determined by his dad.

Bill's recollection was that Nappy was waiting in line to be processed, and that his case was dismissed, and the others were lightly fined. This did not result in the monetary bonanza that the constables and other law enforcement officers anticipated.

In 1960 the United States Supreme Court and the Tennessee legislature eliminated the "fee generating" practice and created the General Sessions Court. Yap became the Circuit Court Clerk in Marion County and served in that capacity for eighteen years.

He is remembered as a helpful public servant to lawyers and citizens who appeared before him and as a powerful politician in local, state and federal races. Both sons freely admit that his Democratic connections impacted their political careers.

One other story about Yap as allegedly told by Jack Wagner, Tax Assessor and later County Executive for Marion County, illustrates his standing in the community. "If someone in a nice suit came into my office and asked me where to find someone, they were always looking for me or another one or two public officials. However, if someone came through that door in poor clothes and had a look on their face that they were down to their last friend, one hundred percent of the time they would ask me where to find Yap!"

Yap also twice tried singer Johnny Cash on charges when the country music legend had a cabin in Haletown near the Tennessee River in Marion County, and they became good friends.

He died on March 5, 2007 survived by his wife of fifty-nine (59) years, Inez and his children and multiple grandchildren and great grandchildren.

ELECTION DAY PRACTICES IN CHATTANOOGA

The history of elections in Chattanooga, Tennessee, might be beneficial to newer members of the municipality's voting public. (It also might jog the recollections of senior citizens).

(1)   With no early voting dates on the calendar, the desire to exercise the privilege to choose one's candidate was often handicapped by long lines, delays, and waits to cast a ballot.

(2)   Although the term "Power Structure" may have changed in meaning in this generation, the ownership of a $100 back tax property lot in the inner city was often placed in the names of prominent residents of the higher elevations of Lookout Mountain, Signal Mountain, Missionary Ridge and Cameron Hill to establish voting residences in Chattanooga.

(3)   The remaining survivors in the subsequent runoffs were quick to seek the support and endorsement of the other non-qualifying office seekers. The losers would all give their public support asking their voters to back their newly chosen candidates "for the good of the City and to move Chattanooga forward under the best leadership." Post-election results would often reveal what political promises and rewards had been made to help their newly backed allies to reach the magic number of 50% (+1) total.

(4)   Until the introduction of television by WDEF in 1954, newspapers, radio and sign companies were the prime beneficiaries of increased revenues during the election cycle.

(5)   The political influence of the two local newspapers the *Chattanooga Times* (Democrat) and the *Chattanooga News-Free Press* (Republican) was demonstrated by many voters simply clipping out the approved slate of candidates by each paper to take to the polls and mark their ballots accordingly.

(6)   Increased church attendance by candidates at various denominations was noted at each election, and additional revenue in the

church offerings was received as each aspiring public servant sincerely or politically attempted to secure the votes of the church attendees in the "Buckle of the Bible Belt." Trucks with ads for a particular candidate were frequently parked across the street from the entrance to what some citizens called the "Power Churches" on Sundays.

Of course, candidates were expected to make a contribution when the offering plate was passed amongst the congregations, irrespective of their religious beliefs or lack of the same.

Prior to the decision in federal court of Brown v. City of Chattanooga in 1989, candidates ran for mayor and commission seats rather than the present mayoral and nine district seats.

The office of Commission of Fire and Police (and others) presented unique opportunities for fund raising amongst the legal and illegal businesses in the city. High ranking police officials often referred to as "bagmen" (no sexist pun intended) often actively used their law enforcement authority to encourage financial support for their boss or candidate (and themselves) in a variety of activities connected to the electoral process.

Whether any remnants of these and other practices remain in operation in Chattanooga today at early voting and election day sites would be a matter of speculation.

CHATTANOOGA CITY ELECTIONS – "ROLLING THE VOTE"

The above term has both national and local implications but generally means efforts of candidates and/or their supporters to get the individual voters to the polls on Election Day.

In years past (and today) candidates would hire vans to transport their prospective voters from nursing homes and individual residences to increase their support. Unfortunately, sometimes the driver of the vans would take money from more than one candidate, and although they would initially transport voters early in the morning, the vans would sometimes not be able to transport voters all day due to alleged vehicle problems or lack of gas by deliberate design. The vans would wind up parked by the side of the road for a while before picking up additional prospective voters for another candidate.

One of the favorite tactics used in City of Chattanooga elections was the use of the "chain ballots."

In the days before liquor by the drink became legal on January 1, 1973, there were establishments in the City of Chattanooga known as "good time" houses where either legal or moonshine shots were available.

In the areas known as "controlled words" a copy of the legitimate ballot was somehow obtained in advance.

Thirsty voters would assemble at one of the houses where they would be given a filled in ballot with the names of the preferred slate of candidates by the political bosses.

The next step would be to transport the prospective voters to the polling place where they would be given a blank ballot by the precinct election officials.

The voters would then enter the privacy curtain and pretend to fill out the ballot while placing the blank one in their pocket. They would then deposit the previously filled in ballot in the voting box.

The last step in this exercise in Democracy would be for the voter to be transported back to the "good time" house where they would be rewarded for their participation in the American electoral process with an alcoholic drink after turning in the blank ballots to the party in charge of disbursing the liquid refreshment.

No wonder that some citizens used to refer to Chattanooga as "Little Chicago!"

JITNEY CABS IN CHATTANOOGA

Before there was Uber and Lyft in Chattanooga, the modes of transportation in the Scenic City were the Yellow Cab Company for fare paying travelers, the Southern Coach Line buses, and the jitney cabs for Negros and for individuals unable to afford a car of their own.

Chattanooga and the State of Tennessee had several periods of problems in public transportation over the issue of segregation on trains and streetcars. On July 5, 1905, Chattanooga blacks staged a street car boycott as the result of segregation being extended to streetcars by the Tennessee legislature under what became known as the "Jim Crowe" law.

Innovative black editor of the *Chattanooga Blade*, Randolph Miller, started the boycott with only lukewarm initial support of black civic and religious leaders. On July 16, Miller and his associates organized black lines boycotting the streetcars and therefore formed the first "jitney cabs" with three vehicles "of sorry appearance" to carry passengers. Initially the first charge for riding in the dilapidated modes of transportation was "5-cent", as this is an archaic name for a "nickel."

Tennessee law described jitney to be "a self-propelling vehicle other than a streetcar traversing the public streets between certain definite points or termini, and as a common carrier, conveying passengers at 5-cent or some small fare between such termini and intermediate points, and so held out, advertised or announced."

No rules or regulations existed in the City Ordinances of the City of Chattanooga prior to February, 1915, when it was reported in the local newspaper that a jitney bus was being operated along Market Street from 6th Street to Main Street. A second entrepreneur placed a large bus into service in the middle of the month and then placed a second bus into operation right after the first. A third competitor had entered the competition on February 4 by putting into operation a 20-passenger vehicle on a scheduled route from downtown to Highland Park and to what was known as the Ridge Junction at Chamberlain and Dobbs Avenue, traveling on McCallie Avenue.

The buses were so profitable that the owner-operator announced that he was going to provide service in the suburb where street car service was provided by the City of Chattanooga. The municipality responded to this unlicensed and unregulated drain on city income, and under the direction of Mayor Thompson, an ordinance was passed regulating fares, routes and taxes.

In April, 1915, the Tennessee legislature joined the controversy by pursing a bill requiring jitney operators to post a bond for each car in operation. This enforcement put one of the operators out of business, but the rise of jitneys continued until another entrepreneur operating the Chattanooga Motor Bus Company petitioned the City Council for an operating license. It was reluctantly granted, but on May 17 the political body attached a number of unacceptable conditions that quickly put the Chattanooga Motor Bus Company out of business.

Over the years, the jitney cabs business fluctuated with economic conditions. Enforcement of the segregations laws was lax, and competition flourished as more jitneys were infiltrating most sections of the city. This caused the Tennessee Electric Power Company (TEPCO) to threaten to go out of business if the City of Chattanooga didn't protect its companies' vested rights by being "its transportation franchise."

Beginning in 1936, battles over the continued existence of the jitney cab system created a wealth of business for the courts and police department that tried unsuccessfully to control the existence of the renegade operation. By the 1930s, white jitney operators had mostly withdrawn from the business. The Tennessee Supreme Court on January 18, 1938, finally settled the question of who had jurisdiction over the regulations of the jitneys when it held that municipalities had the authority to regulate the use of their streets by control over motor carriers within its corporate boundaries.

During World War II, the Southern Coach Lines (SCL) reigned as the designated bona fide franchise of the city. The prosperity of the war resulted in the inability of SCL to provide service for 100,000 daily riders in the system. Therefore the jitney cabs were free to operate without any negative enforcement. However, as business dropped after the end of the war, the SCL called upon the city to take action against the independent operators and to abolish the jitney system.

During the 1950s, there was an ever-growing awareness of the civil rights movement which led to claims of harassment of the black operators. This presented the potential problem of black discontent and violence. During this era, the name of the group of jitney drivers was changed to the Chattanooga Cruising Cab Association as a favorable alternative to "jitney operators."

SCL unsuccessfully tried several tactics in an attempt to drive the new group of operators out of business; an example was changing routes of travel. On June 30, 1971, the Chattanooga Area Regional Transportation Authority (CARTA) was created. In 1973 the Chattanooga Cruising Cab Association approached the city claiming harassment by the new authority. In 1969 a study revealed that there were still 14 jitneys in operation, and in the year 1975 an estimated 1,224,700, passengers were still using the jitney system.

As late as 1977, the fare for riding in a jitney was still 25-cent but was eventually increased to 65-cent which was 5-cents over the CARTA fare of 60-cent. The creation of CARTA, Chattanooga Human Services (HSD) with 37 free vans that included lift-equipped vehicles for wheelchair patients, and the City's Urban Renewal Programs which removed much of the old sub-standard housing along the jitney routs, all contributed to a decline in the number of riders.

A fourth factor that contributed to the demise was the dramatic rise in gasoline prices and vehicle maintenance. Being restricted to taxi stands rather than picking up riders at designated spots also affected the trade as well as lowering wages for the drivers. Nevertheless in the 1980s at least nine independent jitney companies were still picking up the black members of the community along the familiar routes.

History is silent as to when the last surviving jitney cab made its last run in Chattanooga. Today the streets of Chattanooga are clogged with automobiles on pothole-patched streets, as almost totally empty federally-subsidized CARTA buses continue on their skeleton routes.

WINE OF CARDUI = WINE FOR WOMEN

In 1880 Dr. R. I. McElree's Wine of Cardui hit the pharmaceutical market as a menstrual relief product for women. Confident of its anticipated success, the developer of the product made an agreement with the purchasers of the alcohol-laced product that if they were not satisfied with its promised result, they would get their money back. Allegedly 6500 ladies reported being cured of the "vapors" or "fallen womb syndrome," and the company immediately received an additional order of 7000 bottles of the tonic.

The Chattanooga Medicine Company was founded on February 21, 1889, and started operations in an unpretentious two-story brick building on muddy, unpaved Market Street in Chattanooga, Tennessee.

The principal founder of the company was former Union soldier from Illinois, Zeboim Carter Patten. His fellow charter members were H. Clay Evans, Theodore G. Montague, Fred F. Wiehl and Lew Owen who were all successful businessmen in other endeavors.

In 1882 Dr. McElree (he is also referred to as Reverend McElree in some writings) sold his product to the Chattanooga Medicine Company where it was originally marketed as "McElree's Cardui, The Woman's Tonic."

After prohibition passed in 1919-1920, the ingredients were listed as Blessed Thistle, Golden Seal, and 19% alcohol (38 proof). Surprisingly Congress had passed on November 18, 1918, the temporary Wartime Prohibition Act, which banned the sale of alcoholic beverages having an alcohol content of greater than 1.28% (2.56 proof).

When the McElree's Cardui was sold to the Chattanooga Medicine Company, it flourished with sales and profits. In this era women were not the only ones that benefited from the magic elixir. Men had bouts of melancholy, and women suffered from the "vapors," which was described as, "attacks of hysteria, MANIA, clinical depression, bipolar disorder, withdrawal syndrome, fainting, and mood swings of PMS." (Ladies know what this is.)

The main ingredients of this magical tonic were potassium (51.9%), salt (16%) and a varying amount of alcohol that fluctuated up to 23.3% alcohol (46.6 proof).

Prior to hitting the jackpot with Wine of Cardui, the Chattanooga Medicine Company's best seller had been Black Draught Laxative Product, but sales had fallen recently until Wine of Cardui came along and helped the company. Patents to the Black Draught had been bought by Mr. Patten in 1879.

Chattanooga often has been called the "Buckle of the Bible Belt" and the consumption of Wine of Cardui allowed the large teetotaling Baptists, Methodists, and other fundamental religious groups to take Cardui for "medicinal" purposes and remain faithful to their religions.

Some of the advertising materials pertaining to the product are informative with glowing reports from female users:

Mrs. C. M. Ladd wrote, "I take great pleasure in telling you and affected women that I owe my life, my health and my happiness to Wine of Cardui. After my marriage my health broke down and after having tried several physicians and several kinds of medicines, I was given up to die. I had heard of Wine of Cardui and decided to try it. I began to receive benefits at once, and now I am well and strong, and our home has two fine little boys to make it bright and happy."

However the product did have its detractors. Over time the product was analyzed by physicians and was the subject to lawsuits claiming it had no "medicinal value." However it was determined that non-alcoholic ingredients were in large enough quantities to really be medicinal, and it was the 19% alcohol that had an effect on masking the symptoms and making the patients feel better.

In 1916, The Chattanooga Medicine Company, which made Wine of Cardui, brought a successful libel suit against the American Medical Association for its claims that the business was "built on deceit" and that the product was "a vicious fraud." During an adjournment of the court in April 1916, company owner John A. Patten was seized with acute intestinal pain – he was rushed to the hospital and operated on, but unfortunately died.

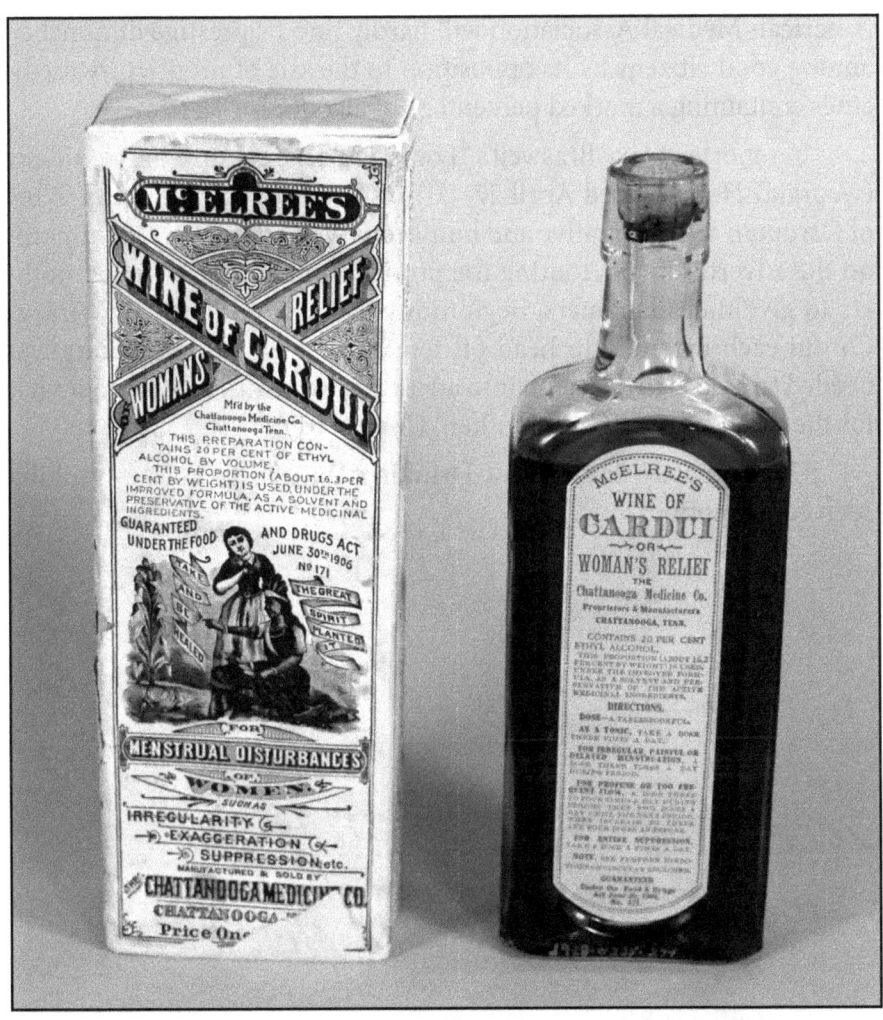

Wine of Cardui manufactured and soild by the Chattanooga Medicie Company

After this unexpected incident, a patent brought by Patten lapsed, but he and his brother had also brought a partnership suit for $100,000, and once the funeral was over, the case continued. The verdict, after the jury had been out a week, was in favor of the Chattanooga Medicine Company – it was awarded damages of one cent. Both sides could claim a victory of sorts. As the *California State Journal of Medicine* pointed out in August 1916, "It is permissible to suggest that the

American Medical Association will hardly find its prestige diminished among good citizens by its opposition to the sale of proprietary medicines containing a marked percentage of alcohol."

In reporter Mary Braswell's "Looking Back" column in the *Albany (Georgia) Herald* dated April 27, 2014, she covers the subject of Wine of Cardui in an informative and humorous way, with several comments on the advertisements touting the production and, "Encourage mothers to give their daughters, beginning at age 12, one dose of Wine of Cardui each morning to head off female problems….. such care was needed to help a girl develop into attractive womanhood and equip her for the duties of a wife and mother." (May 1901)

Unfortunately, the present Drinking Under Age Statues prohibit such consumption.

SPRING CITY-TRAIN-BUS ACCIDENT (1955)

Sometimes good safety practices occur after a tragic accident. A collision between a train and a school bus loaded with children is often devastating to multiple families.

On August 22, 1955 the small rural community of Spring City in the northeast corner of Rhea County was the site of such a fatal collision between a freight train and a Rhea County School bus containing forty-seven students and the bus driver.

In Rhea County, being primarily an agricultural community, schools had started early in the fall in order that the kids living on a farm could be given a week or so as a long break during the harvest season. The town kids would get an extra week out of school also.

At 3:00 p.m. the final school bell rang indicating the end of the school day. The students who rode to school on the bus headed to their bus or one of the other bright yellow vehicles lined up in the school's driveway.

The driver of the bus was a farmer who had started driving a school bus at the beginning of the school year. He would turn left going off school property, and after traveling a couple of blocks, turned right on New Lake Road to head west out of town onto what was then Tennessee State Route 68.

Going west, Route 68 crosses U.S. 27, and about 100 yards further, it crosses the Southern Railway tracks at a signal-protected grade crossing. However sixty five years ago, the crossing consisted of bells and lights without gates. Alternating red lights and the sound of an attention-getting gong were activated when the bus crossed U.S. 27 on the green light. No automatic crossing gate was in existence to prevent the bus from entering on to the track.

The investigation following the crash indicated that the bus driver had unsuccessfully tried to "beat the train" as he tried to make the crossing. The rear end of the bus was struck by a long freight train being pulled by two diesel engines and traveling about 45 miles per hour.

When the engineer saw that the bus was not going to stop before crossing the tracks, he slammed the brakes into full emergency in a desperate attempt to slow down the train, but the lead locomotive tore into the rear half of the bus with a tremendous impact that ripped the bus open.

Ten children were instantly killed and several others were ejected from the bus and sustained serious injuries. An eleventh student later died at the hospital in nearby Rockwood.

The tragic accident had happened in the center of town, only two blocks from the elementary school and one hundred feet from Spring City's main business street, which runs parallel to and on the opposite side of the tracks from U.S. 27.

Emergency medical treatment was very primitive in 1955, but the community responded in a positive manner and transferred the injured in private vehicles to all nearby hospitals in Dayton, Rockwood, Crossville and even Chattanooga, 80 miles away.

Fortunately most of the injured kids recovered, but thirty-one of the students were either killed or injured, leaving only 16 of the 47 on board unhurt. The bus driver, who was unhurt, was charged with involuntary manslaughter and ultimately was tried, convicted and sentenced to one year in jail.

He initially unsuccessfully tried to claim that he stopped the bus before going onto the tracks; several box cars on a nearby railing blocked his view; the signals weren't working; and that the train never blew his horn.

He was released on bond, but due to high community feelings of anger, he had to be placed in protective custody and moved to another town after threats of vigilante street justice were made against him.

None of the driver's excuses were accepted, and Tennessee Governor Frank G. Clement arrived in Spring City and gave a speech at the train depot before a large crowd. He promised a thorough in-depth investigation and personally visited each and every child that was hospitalized.

Due to the public outcry, legislation was drafted which would require every school bus in Tennessee, when transporting children, to stop at all railroad crossings, and for the school bus drivers to actively look and listen for a train and not proceed until the way was safe.

Because of political pressure by the mothers of the slain and injured children and the Spring City Parents Teachers Association (P.T.A.), the new regulations passed the Tennessee General Assembly rapidly. The law became a model for other states, and within a year all forty-eight of the then existing states had enacted their own versions of the bill. It would take over a decade for Congress to pass a version of the bill and to require each state to pass and enforce such a law.

The victims of the crash were initially memorialized with a Memorial Fountain at Spring City Elementary where it stood for fifty years, but it was destroyed when the school was completely reconstructed. On the 50th anniversary (2005) of the crash, a new and larger memorial was erected on the lawn of the city's restored train depot.

The physical presence serves as both a permanent memorial and reminder of the tragedy and the community effort to get laws passed that have probably saved hundreds of lives at school crossings since 1955.

SNAKE HANDLING IN TENNESSEE

The passages in the Bible in Mark 16: 17-18, dealing with the handling of serpents (snakes) and the drinking of any deadly thing (poison) have had historical significance in East Tennessee and Hamilton County. According to the author Thomas Burton in his book *Serpent-Handling Believers*, an in-depth look at snakes and people that handle them, notes that serpents have been associated with religion in some form since ancient, perhaps even pre-historic times. Some Christians in Tennessee believed in and engaged in the practice for many years.

Various Tennessee statutes over the years have attempted to protect the public yet not violate the provisions of Article I, Section 3 of the Tennessee Constitution that advocates the Freedom and Exercise of Religion. A violation of the statute carried a penalty of $50.00-$150.00 fine and up to 6 months imprisonment for endangering the life or health of any person exposed to snakes or reptiles in a dangerous fashion.

The present day penalty for a violation of the snake handling statute only carries a fine of $50.00. Over the years Tennessee and Hamilton County have been the sites of several snake handling episodes, pitting the zealous followers of the practice of snake handling versus law officers attempting to enforce the statutes.

In September 1945, a crowd of approximately 2,500 gathered at the Dolly Pond Church of God in the Grasshopper community off Highway 58 to attend the last rites for preacher Lewis Francis Ford, 32, who had died five days earlier after being bitten by a rattlesnake during a religious ceremony.

Ford had refused medical treatment after being bitten, and his death had made front page news in the Chattanooga newspapers. His death-bed plea was that snakes be handled at his funeral. Hamilton County Sheriff Grady Head insisted that the snakes be handled in a roped off area to avoid accidental bites to spectators. Only "true believers" and reporters and photographers would be allowed inside the ropes.

Six screen-top boxes containing five large rattlesnakes and a copperhead alerted those present with an unsettling buzz of rattler buttons. Prayers followed by "music played by believers with guitars, tambourines, and cymbals" added to the circus atmosphere of the proceedings.

The church members proceeded to chant the words of a strange and rhythmic song followed by one of the members grabbing a four-foot rattlesnake. Speaking in an unknown tongue, he placed the reptile around his shoulders. This was followed by other congregation members grabbing snakes form the boxes and passing them around.

One of the handlers seized a long black rattler and shouted to the crowd, "This is the one that killed our brother (Ford)." Then he threw the serpent into the open casket containing the decedent's corpse.

Ford had been bitten by a snake at a service near Daisy in north Hamilton County. The snake sank its fangs into Ford's finger, but he continued preaching for another ten minutes before he fell ill. Refusing medical treatment, he was dead within three hours. Ford was buried in the first grave in the Dolly Pond Church of God Cemetery.

Approximately a year later, three snake handlers in the Cleveland, Tennessee, area died from snakebites.

In 1975 the Tennessee Supreme Court accepted a case out of Newport, Tennessee, to determine whether the State of Tennessee could enjoin (stop) a religious group from handling snakes as a part of its religion in accordance with the Articles of Faith of the church, on the basis of such action constituting a public nuisance. The high court held that the practice could be banned if the handling of the snake endangered the life or health of any person.

In January 2014, the Tennessee Wildlife Resources Agency (TWRA) attempted to prosecute Pastor Andrew Hamblin of the Tabernacle Church of God in Lafollette, Tennessee, on charges related to the possession of illegal deadly snakes deemed by the TWRA agents to be dangerous to the public. After a preliminary hearing in the General Sessions Court, the charges were sent to the Campbell County Grand

Jury which refused to indict Hamblin although he admitted to having 53 venomous snakes at his church.

Thus the law in Tennessee is still in dispute as to whether the handling of serpents is a matter of faith under the freedom of speech provision of the Tennessee Constitution or protection of the pubic under a state statute.

CHATTANOOGA'S NEGRO LEAGUE NINES

With 2020 being the 100th Anniversary of the origin of African-American national professional baseball leagues in 1920, the year has resulted in additional historical interest in black baseball teams.

Although informal semi-pro and professional Negro ball teams had been in existence since the 1880s, it was not until 1920 that the Negro National League was formed. Several other leagues were created over the years but most were short lived because of financial problems.

The Atlanta Braves at Truist Park Baseball Stadium in 2020 televised segments on black baseball history on their cable broadcasts of each game and have included many black players in their history areas at the stadium.

Kansas City, Missouri, is the home of the Negro League Baseball Museum which was established in 1990 and is dedicated to preserving the rich history of African-American baseball.

Chattanooga reportedly fielded its first team in 1886 in the earliest Negro League in the country known as the Southern League of Colored Base Ballists.

Over the years numerous black teams existed in the Scenic City such as Chattanooga Chatts (1889-1892); Chattanooga Warriors (1893); Chattanooga Unions (1901); Chattanooga (1909-1910); Chattanooga Black Lookouts I (1920); Chattanooga Tigers (1921-1923); Chattanooga White Sox (1926); Chattanooga Choo-Choos (1940-1948); Chattanooga All Stars (1949); Chattanooga Black Choo-Choos (1950) and Chattanooga Stars (1951).

In addition to playing in leagues, the teams also engaged in "barnstorming" tours playing road games in selective cities throughout the country as special events that often drew large crowds.

Segregation restrictions in informal agreements between white baseball owners prevented African Americans from playing in the better-known and better financial white leagues. The "Gentlemen's Agreement" in the 1920s would lead to the banning of black players from major league baseball until 1947 when Jackie Robinson broke the color restriction with the Brooklyn Dodgers.

Black and white teams did compete in barnstorming games together traveling from city to city playing in unofficial games.

The story of barnstorming was told in the movie, *The Bingo Long Traveling All-Stars and Motor Kings* (1976) featuring Billy Dee Williams, James Earl Jones and Richard Pryor.

Chattanooga was the start of the careers of two of the greatest players in the history of the Negro Leagues who later played Major League Baseball.

The legendary Leroy "Satchel" Paige, who is often considered the greatest pitcher of all time (black and white), first played for the Chattanooga Black Lookouts in 1926. Paige was hired at a salary of $250 a month of which he allegedly kept $50 and sent the rest home to his mother. He was the first pitcher from the old Negro League to be elected to the National Baseball Hall of Fame.

His nickname of "Satchel" may have been created when he arrived in Chattanooga with a few clothes in a brown grocery sack.

In 1948 he would become the first black ballplayer in the American League when he pitched for the Cleveland Indians while at an unconfirmed age in his 50s.

Future Hall of Famer outfielder Willie Mays first played for the Chattanooga Choo Choos as an infielder in 1946. His mother and father divorced over their disagreement as to whether he should sign to play baseball at the age of 16 or stay in high school.

One writer reports that Jackie Robinson also played for the Chattanooga Choo Choos, but a search of the Baseball Almanac records lists him as playing only one season in the Negro League for the Kansas City Monarchs in 1945.

The publication also reports that he played shortstop in that year's Negro League All Star Game and did great in the field but went zero-for-five at bat.

He was the first black player to win election to the National Baseball Hall of Fame in 1962.

Many other great black players such as Josh Gibson and "Cool" Papa Bell never had the opportunity to play major league baseball, but they and many others have been acclaimed as being equally great players by white players that competed against them.

Joe DiMaggio and Floyd (Babe) Herman said that Satchel Paige was the toughest pitcher they had ever faced.

Baseball in Chattanooga's history has been color blind with great players performing at all of the historical baseball fields at Andrews Field, Lincoln Park, Engel Stadium, Bell South Park and AT&T Field.

GLENWOOD MANOR – EDUCATIONAL ACADEMY?

Down Dodds Avenue at the western base of Missionary Ridge, at the corner of McCallie Avenue, a block from a prominent male prep school and the former site of the campus of the relocated Central High School, is the location of a former institution of non-accredited learning about the facts of life that some young men from both schools acquired. These lessons were not part of the regular curriculum of young male high school students.

All that exists now to identify its location is a non-functioning rusting neon sign.

In the 1940s – 1960s the sign glowed brightly as a welcome beacon to the young men and adults that were willing to part with a few dollars to learn further knowledge of the "oldest profession" known to man.

Glenwood Manor's social history is documented in the legal annuals of Tennessee jurisprudence in a published case located at 352 S.W.2d 227 (1961). The middle aged madam was charged and indicted on a charge of operating a bawdy house and unlawfully engaging in assignation. She was tried before a Hamilton County trial jury and was fined the astronomical amount of $50.00 in the first charge and $25.00 on the second.

The record shows that on or about February 11, 1961, the ever-vigilant Chattanooga Police Department began an investigation of the Glenwood Manor by placing it under surveillance by a uniformed police officer. He observed the motel on several occasions during which time he saw men, alone, in pairs or in small groups and men and women in couples, enter the motel at all times of the night staying from 30 minutes to 2 hours and leaving. The female defendant lived in the motel and used it as her home and as a motel. She also provided other illegal and educational services.

Testimony from a neighbor was that most of the visitors to the motel arrived and departed in cars or taxi cabs bearing Hamilton

County, Tennessee license plates. The investigation intensified when the same neighbor stated that his family had been disturbed frequently with profane talk and excessive activity around the motel, and that it had a reputation in the community of being a "bawdy house."

In order to crack down and eliminate a major criminal enterprise, the Chattanooga Police Department sent in a handsome young officer to do some "undercover" work and to rent a room for five days.

The officer observed unusual activities for a legitimate motor-lodge and engaged the proprietor in conversation about the extent of services to the public.

She told the young man that she "dated" and also told him that she could supply any number of dates by her and her friends for a price of approximately $15.00 each (negotiable rate).

During his week-long sabbatical from more strenuous police work, he saw women come to the motel and leave the motel escorted and unescorted by men.

After additional undercover police work by two more officers posing as potential clients, and establishing a price of $60.00 for the joint companionship of the madam and another lady, a search warrant was executed and the motel was raided. The madam was found to be completely undressed and her companion was partially unclad.

A defense of entrapment was unsuccessful and the proprietor and assistant were convicted.

Unfortunately this did not end the efforts of the madam to continue her career of educating the male public of the values of her craft, as she was convicted once again for an act of prostitution in 1968 during the twilight years of her career.

A law-and-order-minded trial jury this time fined the business woman the sum of $50.00.

Although Chattanooga does not have the best record of preserving historical relics, it is hopeful that some public minded citizen should purchase or at least refurbish the now decaying neon sign outside the Glenwood motel to light up this symbol of the free enterprise system in Chattanooga. An elder graduate from either of the two high schools might even pay for the repair of this treasure from the past. (With a chuckle or at least a smile!)

P.S. The madam who operated the establishment has been heard by witnesses to proudly exclaim that she had graduated from a conservative church university in Spartenburg, South Carolina, but no witness can verify that she displayed a graduation diploma on any of the walls of the brothel.

MIDDLE TENNESSEE MULE DAY

Columbia, Tennessee prides itself as being the "Mule Capital" of the world and yearly puts on a four day celebration that attracts in excess of 200,000 participants and spectators.

What started in 1940 as "Breeders Day" for a meeting for mule breeders has evolved into a full schedule featuring traditional Appalachian food, music, dancing and with arts and crafts items for sale.

The 80-year event concludes with the Mule Day Parade on Saturday as the highlight of the festivities. A variety of activities are held at various locations.

Each day's events start at 7:00 with a choice of breakfast fare including ham and biscuits and pancakes. Throughout the day, barbecue, roasted corn, home-made pies and funnel cakes are served.

Competition events including log loading, feed time race, beard growing, pony mule pulling and mule pulling. Other events include "working mule", "best of breed" and "lumberjack" competitions.

The annual "mule pull" contest requires a pair of mules to pull a sled loaded with cinder blocks a distance of ten feet. Each pair of mules is given three tries to make it the full ten feet. The team that pulls the most weight wins the competition.

The dedicated involvement of the Maury County community in the mule industry has caused the event to grow into "one of the largest livestock markets in the world."

In 1934 the first "Mule Day Parade" was held on Saturday and involved a competition for the best decorated floats for cash or ribbon prizes. The idea for the Mule Day Parade came from an individual by the name of Thomas Marion Brown, and with the support of the local Chamber of Commerce and the local *Daily Herald* newspaper, the parade became a part of the celebration.

Brown is credited with designing the original Mule Day Crown worn by the "Mule Day Queen" selected on the basis of the quality of an essay and other criteria for contestants between the ages of 15-21. A queen and her court will be selected, will attend all Mule Day events, and will be interviewed by local radio stations and newspapers. They will make a trip to the State Capitol in Nashville to participate in more interviews by the media to promote the Mule Day celebration.

Tom Brown also served as the Grand Marshall of the Mule Day Parade for the first seven years. Over the years celebrities such as University of Tennessee at Knoxville coaches Pat Summit and Phil Fulmer, plus 2000 Miss U.S.A., Lynette Cole, have served as Grand Marshall of the Saturday parade. In 2019 Channel 2 News Anchor Neil Orne from Nashville was selected Grand Marshall.

A new event was added in 2015 on Wednesdays. It is an auction for the sale of mules at Maury County Park conducted by the Lewisburg Livestock Market.

Over the years the celebration has become a "don't miss" event for politicians in office or aspiring to become elected to a public office in Tennessee.

Although the 2020 event was canceled because of the COVID-19 epidemic by the joint decision of the Maury County Bridle and Saddle Club and the City of Columbia and Maury County government, plans for the 2021 event are underway.

Information can be obtained from the Mule Day Office, P.O. Box 66, Columbia, TN 38402, (931) 381-9557, www.muleday.com, e-mail: info@muleday.com

HALES BAR – GHOST INHABITED SITE

We have previously written about the ghosts that resided at Brushy Mountain Penitentiary in Petros and South Pittsburg's haunted hospital in Marion County. However, the closest site to Chattanooga for the paranormal fans is the Hales Bar Marina.

I have been informed that the haunted spirits will be communicating with any citizens brave enough to venture on the premises at 1265 Hales Bar Road, Guild, Tennessee 37340. Details can be obtained by leaving a phone message at (423) 942-9000 or going on the web at www.halesbarmarina.com. From the website it seems they have various guest speakers during October, and plans include vendors, food, soft drinks, and beer at their cash bar. Tickets should be ordered ahead.

The history of Hales Bar Dam has been well documented. It is a vital part of the history of the Tennessee River. Prior to the building of the Nickajack Dam near Shellmound in Marion County, the effort to curb the often-raging river was the facility at Hales Bar. Before Hales Bar Dam, the Tennessee River was once a major source of danger to year-round traffic in the Tennessee River Gorge.

There were three whirlpool areas knows as "The Suck," "The Skillet" and "The Pan," with "The Suck" being the most dangerous. These sites also had paranormal reputations. The Indians that originally lived in the area prior to the "Trail of Tears" claimed that they could see the souls of their ancestors being sucked into the massive whirlpool.

In 1905 after a favorable site had been approved by the U.S. Army Corps of Engineers, construction started at Hales Bar which was an economic boom to the community. Joseph Conn Guild, an engineer from Chattanooga, lobbied Congress for the authorization to raise funds to build the dam in exchange for the rights to the dam's hydroelectric output to the public and communities. Guild then formed the Chattanooga and Tennessee River Power Company later known as TEPCO. Two self-contained communities, Guild (Haletown) and Ladd were created to accommodate the thousands of workers necessary to erect the dam.

Hales Bar power house on the Tennessee River

Legend also included the presence of some angry Indian spirits who were upset because the water where the dam was being built was sacred. War Chief Dragging Canoe cursed this land on March 17, 1775, during the illegal Treaty of Sycamore Shoals.

Problems arose during the construction of the dam when it was discovered that it was being built on a weak limestone foundation. Leakage would remain a problem for forty years. Although originally scheduled to start producing electricity in 1909, it was not able to commence operation until November 13, 1913, at a cost of $10,000,000 instead of the original estimation of $2,000,000.

Prior to the adoption of the OSHA (Occupational Safety Health Administration) which was enacted by Congress on December 29, 1970, working conditions were very dangerous with limited safety rules to protect workers on projects such as Hales Bar.

As a result, there were many deaths and bad injuries on the site. This has likewise led to more paranormal stories about construction and mason workers who helped build Hales Bar Dam and were killed and are buried within the concrete wall and never recovered. Their spirits still haunt the premises. One of those spirits is the ghost of a murdered woman whose body was buried in the concrete walls and she is still present.

In 1967 the federal government finished Nickajack Dam that replaced Hales Bar Dam and left only the massive control house on the shore of the river. The Control house is the location of the paranormal experiences.

Marion County provides potential "ghostbusters" the opportunity to exercise their urge to visit the spiritual world at either the haunted hospital in South Pittsburg or the likewise haunted power house at Hales Bar. Both are just a short drive off I-24.

Reservations can be made for the various events scheduled during October and in the following months throughout the year. The aptly named "6 Fears Hells Bar Dam" ticket sales end November 1. For the additional sum of $6.00 your group can even purchase your own "Ghost Meter" and search for paranormal activity at Hales Bar.

Who knows? The Ghosts of Halloween may be present!

PINE BREEZE SANATORIUM
(1909-1968)

The luxury River Point development now stands on the site of the former Pine Breeze Sanatorium on Stringer's Ridge in Hamilton County, Tennessee.

The history of Pine Breeze is filled with stories of the treatment of patients suffering from tuberculosis (TB), mentally disturbed juveniles, and paranormal stories of satanic activities.

Pine Breeze treated many patients for TB from its inception in 1909 when it was chartered, and to its closure in 1968 and conversion to other uses. TB has pretty much been eradicated through the invention of drugs that have been called "magical."

Throughout history TB which was once called "consumption" is an infectious bacterial disease that has plagued mankind. Tennessee was once ranked as one of the leading states in incidence of TB cases, and Hamilton County was often ranked as the number one TB County in the State.

Pine Breeze initially was a place where people were sent to die because of TB. A book titled *The Road From Pine Breeze* (2010) by author Elizabeth Long on Amazon.com tells the true life story of Jo Price, who entered Pine Breeze when she was 16 years old suffering from advanced TB in both lungs. She was placed in the terminal wing known as "death row!" Her story of her experiences while she was at the sanatorium is gripping and shocking. Her 2009 interview with local historian Harmon Jolley and the contents in her book relate a painful journey that probably only a person with a strong Christian faith could have endured.

The bright red brick buildings often bely what happened at Pine Breeze. The gloomy description of the premises by Mrs. Price and the administration of multiple hypodermic shots through the rib cage and into the pleura cavity and through the stomach every few hours sound

A postcard of Pine Breeze

Pine Breeze, Paul A. Hiener Collection

like a form of torture from the middle ages but was the prescribed form of treatment during the 1940s – 1960s.

Streptomycin was then the drug of choice but had to be given in the form of a shot every six hours for four months. Eventually a drug called para amigo slicic acid (pas) was developed and helped eradicate (or control) TB in the United States.

With the curing of TB the hospital fell into inactivity and closed in 1968, but in the late 1960s, it re-opened for the purpose of treating emotionally disturbed children. It was known as Pine Breeze Center and was used in that capacity until 1981-1982 when the juvenile patients were transferred to Moccasin Bend Mental Health Institute.

With the closing of the sanatorium came the usual ghost stories about spirits that still haunt the premises in spite of the new luxury complex.

Whether fact or fiction, reports of mental patients being chained to the walls, and the presence of a pentagram on the floor of one of the abandoned buildings in the 1990s made from broken chunks of concrete and white stone have been told.

Further reports of red substances (that looked like blood), unreadable words written on the walls, and rumors of goats being sacrificed by "Satanists" have been conveyed by teenagers who have visited the premises to drink alcoholic beverages or to "turn on" by the use of drugs.

Around 1995 the buildings were demolished and the luxury development emerged.

Whether any spirits from Pine Breeze have presented themselves to any of the new owners has yet to be disclosed, but who knows what might happen on a cold damp and wet night at the former site known as Pine Breeze?

One historical remnant to the past of Pine Breeze is the recording of musical songs led by a young college graduate, Ron Williams, in 1975. He started working at Pine Breeze as a teacher, counselor and supervising the juveniles in the dormitory at the facility. Williams came up with the idea of recording music from local musicians in the area to preserve tunes that may have originated as far back as the 1920s.

Most of the musicians that were taped were not professionals who earned a living from playing music. They enjoyed playing at Chattanooga's old-time fiddle contests, square dances and community events.

The song "Old Chattanooga" was recorded by a trio of Pine Breeze patients, and Ron Williams relates that it is very popular and well-known on present-day social media and YouTube.

Maybe on some cold dreary night the sounds of the song may be heard across the grounds of the former medical facility for TB patients and mentally disturbed juveniles?

THE SUCK

Boaters headed towards the Tennessee River Gorge aka "Grand Canyon of Tennessee" from Chattanooga to enjoy the fall foliage will have to pass the mouth of Suck Creek and will have little or no difficulty navigating through the historical area known as "The Suck."

That was not always the case prior to the erection of the Hales Bar Dam by the Tennessee River Power Company (TEPCO) headed by Chattanooga engineer Joseph Conn Guild, and the Chickamauga Dam up the Tennessee River in the late 1930's and 1940's. Hales Bar Dam construction started in 1905. Two nearby towns of Guild (now known as Haletown) and Ladds were built to house the thousands of workers that were needed to build the dam.

On November 1, 1913, the dam was completed at a cost of $237,000,000 in todays value but had a checkered past with leaks and deaths of workers and private citizens.

After the Tennessee Valley Authority (TVA) was passed in 1933, litigation occurred as to the constitutionality of the law which gave TVA the right to buy the assets of Hales Bar Dam for $78,000,000. The location of "the Suck" southwest of Chattanooga consisted of strong currents and whirlpools that were hazards and dangerous to any boats trying to transverse the area.

Just before the start of the Civil War and through 1886, steamboats were a popular mode of transportation on the Tennessee River. Because the water level at "the Suck" was so low that the riverboats drafted too deep to get through the area, it became necessary to dredge out where Suck Creek flowed into the river. Even after the dredging to make the river deeper, the steamboats still had difficulty navigating this area when it rained heavily because Suck Creek would spill large amounts of water into the river. That caused a suction which made it very difficulty for the steamboats to get through.

Several dangerous spots soon acquired colorful names by the local inhabitants such as Tumbling Shoals, the Pot, the Skillet, and the

Pan and each became difficult for rivermen to avoid the downstream journey hazards and also restricted upstream travel. The idea of building human-powered winches on the shorelines to go to the bow of the steamboats was developed. Slaves turned the giant wooden winches in order to pull the large boats through "the Suck."

With the erecting of the Hales Bar Dam, water levels in Chattanooga rose permanently. Today the area is relatively quiet compared to older times, but some whirls still exist. In 1964 construction began on Nickajack Dam, six miles downstream from Hales Bar Dam. It was completed in 1967 at a cost of $73,000,000, and Hales Bar was taken out of service, and the dam portion was removed.

It's hard to imagine the difficulty of going through the three-hundred-yard section of the river at this point, but it took the Hales Bar Dam to control the rapid current that made the passage through "the Suck" so difficult that steamboats had to be pulled by human labor with the winches.

The Suck obtained historical notoriety when country music icon Johnny Cash recorded the ballad, "The Whirl and the Suck."

GHOSTS OF SEWANEE

Although the accounts of paranormal experiences have recently evolved into tourist attraction locations at abandoned prisons and various other sites, experiences with ghosts have occurred much longer at the University of the South at Sewanee atop the Cumberland Plateau.

Beginning as far back as November 1892 (or earlier) in Sewanee's annual *Cap and Gown*, and the student newspaper, *Sewanee Purple*, there have been a number of stories printed in the publications about ghosts at Sewanee. There were ghost stories about "a crying baby, headless dogs, ghostly gownsmen, headless gownsman, footsteps following people, a professor walking, and a foaming black horse running by people at night."

Resident Dave Short encountered a ghost near the old stage coach road. He heard a baby crying and went over to see about it. He saw a red-headed baby wrapped in a blanket lying in the underbrush. He stooped over to pick it up, but it suddenly disappeared. His brothers, Reuben and Ed Short, were afraid to go out with him at night, since strange things seemed to happen in his presence. Other mountain residents have said that strange things have happened near the old stage coach road, too.

Actually there have been so many ghostly sightings on the Sewanee Mountain that, "It seems to be a ghost haven!"

In the 1892 *Cap and Gown* article, it mentions the "ghost that rides the foaming black horse and goes dashing by the inoffensive midnight wanderer." (Whether the wanderer is a descendant of Icabod Crane depicted in Washington Irvin's *The Legend of Sleepy Hollow* in 1820 is not addressed).

Another spirit is mentioned in the same article about "the much talked about overactive little white-robed child that wanders aimlessly in and out of the upper chapel gate - 'the baby that crawls.'"

The advent of the Ghost of Wyndcliff Hall (now gone) relates the tale of a Headless Gownsman (attire of Sewanee students) that appeared before six students in the School of Theology. Allegedly one student was encouraged to stop studying by the other students, but he refused, and an argument ensued which resulted in a pillow fight that resulted in the student's head rolling off his body.

The explanation for said action was, "The unlucky youth had studied too hard and outweighed his brains with the dismal result."

Efforts of the unlucky student to retrieve his head were unsuccessful and the scholar was unable to "overtake his errant noodle." As the head tumbled down the stairs it produced a bump-bump-bump sound that continued to reverberate throughout the Wyndcliff Hall during its existence. The Head was especially active during mid-term exams.

Other Sewanee ghosts include the "Headless Dog" and the "Perambulating Professor."

The Headless Dog regularly walked between the present printing office and the Palmetto House. The dog was white as to body but lacked a head. It is alleged that a student struck it with a cane on what should have been the head of the animal, and he never completely received from the shock of finding only empty space.

The Perambulating Professor liked to accompany any student that took any late-at-night walk to Green's View. The spirit was a social ghost, although a silent one.

A fraternity house was also haunted. It made no difference that after a chapter meeting and everything had been cleaned up, the next morning there would always be at least four chairs at the table and "a subtle odor that suggested the nocturnal presence of departed spirits."

The 1921 edition of the *Cap and Gown* annual reported that the "Crying Baby" ghost haunted the old chapel steps and cried and wailed in a chilling voice.

The story of another spirit arose out of the athletic contests between Sewanee and Vanderbilt. The two schools had developed a tradition of playing a football game the week before Thanksgiving. It was reported that every year after Sewanee had defeated her Nashville rival, a "baby" was heard to cry somewhere on the campus each night exactly at midnight. In 1924 a crowd of students, residents and faculty had assembled on Thursday night before the traditional game and had waited in the unlighted chapel where the spirit resided. The crowd grew on each subsequent midnight to hear the "crying baby" waiting to predict a victory on the gridiron. The chapel was crowded and students were "standing on the roof, in every possible part of the chapel inside and outside."

Outside the year 1924 the "baby" has not cried, and ironically Sewanee did not defeat Vanderbilt in football since that fall, and the series between the rivals ended.

In 1997 local resident Patricia Short Makris wrote an interesting history of Sewanee, *The Other Side of Sewanee*, that includes additional ghost stores and ghosts on the domain.

Whether real or fictional, the stories of "ghosts" at Sewanee provide more fascination to the intriguing history of the University of the South.

LINCOLN PARK – VITAL AFRICAN AMERICAN LANDMARK

When a resident of a community uses the term "gentrification" most readers scurry to the dictionary to ascertain what the term means. It has been defined as "a process of changing the character of a neighborhood through the influence of more affluent residents and businesses." It has also been a frequent and controversial topic in urban planning and politics.

Some residents of the Lincoln Park community allege that the term should be applied to the encroachment of apartment developers and Erlanger Hospital and the longtime proposal to extend Central Avenue to deprive them of the historical heritage of Lincoln Park. Others claim that just the opposite is true, and that property owners are treating renters fairly.

Lincoln Park first opened on June 1, 1918 as Chattanooga's first park for black residents. Ten acres had been purchased by the City of Chattanooga and Hamilton County to build an isolated wing at Erlanger Hospital but the site was instead changed to a recreational area for blacks that lived in the neighborhood at the rear of the hospital.

In that era of segregation blacks were precluded from using the city's popular Warner Park facilities which were open only to white residents. The initial plans for the park "were to include a children's playground, a dancing pavilion, a carousel, a refreshment stand and restrooms for men and women."

It was not until 1937 that a community swimming pool was approved, constructed and dedicated in 1938.

In 1946 Lincoln Park further expanded with the erection of a round building named the Lincoln Center.

In 1947 a huge Fourth of July celebration was held in a highly advertised event that drew bus-loads of black tourists from Atlanta, Nashville, and other major cities in the South.

A small zoo consisting of monkeys and a bear was a popular attraction, as was a Ferris wheel.

Important in the history of Lincoln Park is the lighted baseball field. Black baseball games were played on two days of the week. Before Engel Stadium was built in 1929, black baseball teams played their games at Andrews Field and Lincoln Park.

Lincoln Park was the home field of the Chattanooga Black Cats during the 1929 season, and another black team, the Chattanooga Choo Choos played at Lincoln Park. Future Hall of Famer Willie Mays played for the team in the 1940s, and Satchel Paige and maybe Jackie Robinson played on the field during its heyday. Today only the baseball field, a concession stand, and a part of the pool entrance are about all that remains of this historical area.

With the onset of desegregation in the 1960s attendance at the park dropped, and the City of Chattanooga decided to give its financial support to Warner Park.

Urban renewal and hospital expansion (Erlanger) took place in the 1950s and 1960s which again changed and reduced further the Lincoln Park acreage.

As a sign of things to come, the City of Chattanooga traded the Lincoln Park property to Erlanger for land in Glenwood where the children's hospital was once located.

Some residents argue that ever since the 1980s, Erlanger Hospital and the City of Chattanooga have tried to reduce the residential space in Lincoln Park. Any planned expansion of Central Avenue will run through Lincoln Park and destroy the historical baseball field.

Such action has not gone unnoticed. Citizens groups as Chattanooga Organized for Actions, Coalition to Save Lincoln Park, and the Lincoln Park Neighborhood Association have been created to continue the fight against any effort of Chattanooga to expand the Central Avenue through Lincoln Park.

Two papers adequately state the history of Lincoln Park and merit the consideration of interested readers. "Research Report: Lincoln Park in Chattanooga, Tennessee" by Sarah Calise dated December 9, 2015, (21 pages) and "Negro Removal in Chattanooga" by associate professor, Dr. Ken Chilton, of Tennessee State University, released on January 12, 2019 (17 pages) recently address the pluses and minuses of the history of Lincoln Park. Both can be retrieved in their entirety by googling Google Chrome. Chilton did remark, "The benefits of Chattanooga's renaissance have not trickled down."

In 2019 the Chattanooga City Council approved an expenditure of Two Million Dollars ($2,000,000) for upgrades at the park. The effectiveness and use of that appropriation is beyond the scope of this article....

It does appear that it will be one of the issues to be discussed by the residents of District 8 presently represented by Councilman Anthony Byrd in 2021.

The preservation of Lincoln Park may determine whether the use of the term "gentrification" is to be further applied to another historical area of our community?

BRUSHY MOUNTAIN PENITENTIARY – ALCATRAZ TENNESSEE?

What was once Tennessee's most infamous prison that included inmates such as James Earl Ray, killer of Martin Luther King, and Byron "Low Tax" Looper, assassin of State Senator Tommy Burks, is now a popular tourist stop at Petros, in Morgan County, fifty miles from Knoxville.

Two Chattanooga entrepreneurs, Brian May and Pete Warrington, leased the penitentiary and re-opened it in 2018. The stone structure was built in the 1930s by prisoners after an 1896 wooden building burned. The prison was built from stone dug from a quarry on the property. Those prisoners also built a railroad spur, worked in coal mines on the site, operated coke ovens or farmed.

The selection of Brushy Mountain in the rugged hill county was based on the goal of making it a maximum-security prison that would be very difficult from which to escape. This turned out to be true because the escape plans of James Earl Ray and six other inmates who climbed over the fence in 1977 were thwarted by the rough terrain. The fugitives were apprehended two days later a few miles from the prison.

One temporary escape story was of convicted kidnapper and murderer, James Slage who had become a student of yoga and packed himself in a shipping crate labeled "153 pounds of roast beef" that went out of the prison on a flatbed truck. Unfortunately, his absence was soon discovered and he was apprehended.

Initially the prisoners were convict lease laborers, but when those arrangements expired in 1896, two hundred ten of those prisoners became the first inmates of Brushy Mountain.

In 1972, after a strike by prison guards protesting unsafe working conditions, the prison was closed that year and re-opened in 1976. Governor Lamar Alexander attempted to defeat the group that was the only unionized prison in the state but was unsuccessful as the bargaining unit worked hard with legislators in Nashville to improve working conditions.

In the 1980s as more prisons were built due to overcrowding, Brushy changed from a maximum security prison and became a classification facility with a reduced inmate capacity of 584. It became the East Tennessee reception/classification and diagnostic center. Although it was no longer a maximum-security institution, a separate annex within the prison temporarily housed up to 96 beds for Tennessee's most troublesome inmates.

Ultimately the prison closed on July 11, 2009 and its functions were transferred to the Morgan County Correctional Complex to which it had been administratively joined.

For literary fans, Brushy has been referred to in several movies, television shoes and novels. Anthony Hopkins as Dr. Hannibal Lecter in the film, "The Silence of the Lambs" offered to inform on the Serial Killer Buffalo Bill if they "would send him to Brushy."

In the popular 1991 John Grisham novel, *The Firm*, the brother of Mitch McDeere, played by Tom Cruise, was an inmate at Brushy Mountain, named Ray McDeere. The late singer, John Hiatt's 1988 song "Tennessee Plates" main character lamented about being in "the Tennessee prison up in Brushy Mountain = making Tennessee plates." (making license plates was one of the vocational jobs at Brushy.)

Morgan county elected officials were unsuccessful in converting the old prison to other uses including a museum and jail to serve Morgan and adjoining counties.

Up to 2012 the prison was vacant and abandoned until Chattanooga entrepreneur Pete Waddington saw the facility on a charity motorcycle ride through Morgan County. Astounded by what he saw and recognizing the possibilities, he contacted his fellow Chattanoogan Brian May. They leased the Brushy Mountain property, and they have turned it into a tourist attraction.

Normally from April - December the tourist center is open but due to the Corona-virus it is closed until allowed to re-open by the

Tennessee Moonshine marketed as "End of the Line" is legally distilled at the former Brushy Mountain prison and is available for testing and purchase.

government. Because of the lack of heat due to the cold weather, the facility is not open in the winter.

Tours with guides who are either former guards or inmates are available or you can tour on your own. If you are really brave and love ghost stories, a paranormal tour is available for groups up to 12, if you can stand being locked up from 11:00 p.m. to 6:00 a.m. or for how long you can stay in the prison.

The "Warden's Table" is a restaurant serving barbecue, salads, hamburgers, etc. and there is also a gift shop. An 18 minute documentary runs continuously at various locations three times an hour.

May and Waddington have provided an amenity that even Alcatraz in San Francisco Bay can't match. Their "End of the Line" Tennessee Moonshine and Frozen Head Vodka are legally distilled at the prison and available for testing and purchase. The museum includes a variety of "old records, photos, news articles and prison artifacts" that were confiscated from prisoners.

In 2018 a concert drew 4,000 fans, and the owners hope to schedule a monthly music series.

Information can be obtained about Brushy at:
Phone – 423-324-8687
Location – 9182 Highway 116, Petros, Tennessee
Details – https://tourbrushy.com/

Who knows? Brushy may someday be known as "Tennessee's Alcatraz!"

P.S. The facility is now open for business.

DOLLY PARTON AND THE GREASY POLE

The stories about country and pop superstar, Dolly Parton and how Cas Walker gave her the first singing job on radio and television are well known. At the age of ten she became a regular on his early morning television show on WBIR-TV in Knoxville, and Dolly credits Cas with giving her a start in her career.

However one story is both acknowledged and denied by acquaintances of Cas and Dolly. After she started appearing on Cas' radio and television shows, she also was expected to perform at live shows in surrounding areas. Cas had rented a place in Sevierville, Tennessee and would put on live music shows.

One of his gimmicks to raise crowds was to take a fifty foot long wooden pole, dig a hole in the ground and then put the pole in it and surround it with concrete around the bottom. The pole would be covered with grease, and before the pole was installed in the ground Cas would attach fifty $50 dollars on top. Every Saturday the contest drew a large crowd to see if any contestant could climb the pole and get the cash without sliding off of it before they could get the money.

According to one story Dolly had tried to climb the pole every weekend when she was six years old in a pair of overalls but couldn't make it to the top. Finally, one Saturday she allegedly had her mother take her down to the river and Dolly waded out and got wet. She then rolled in a sandbar and had grit and sand all over her clothes. With this sand on her clothes she was able to climb the pole and get Cas' fifty dollars and end his greasy pole contest.

Another acquaintance Larry Mathis refuted the story and claimed that neither Dolly nor anyone else ever climbed the greasy pole although a great many people tried and that it was a great crowd attraction. Larry and several of his friends make the same assertion that no one ever climbed that pole and nearly all of them are dead.

Dolly may be the only survivor that can verify Cas' claim that she climbed the greasy pole as he expressed in his autobiography, *Cas Walker, My Life Story*.

ALABAMA ARTICLES

MENTONE SPRINGS HOTEL

The once stately Mentone Springs Hotel in Mentone, Alabama, in DeKalb County, southwest of Chattanooga is now silent with only a vacant lot and a "for sale" sign where the once popular resort stood.

On March 1, 2014, an electrical fire destroyed the one hundred and thirty-year-old Mentone Springs Hotel along with an antique mall on the property. The hotel had been built by physician Dr. J. Frank Caldwell from Pennsylvania in 1884-1887. He had become fond of the area when he had vacationed there.

The name of the hotel came from the daughter of a local resident, John Mason, who Dr. Caldwell had lived with while the 28,000 square foot structure was being erected. The daughter, Alice, recalled reading descriptive accounts of British monarch, Queen Victoria, who had visited a place in France called Mentone. The meaning of Mentone had been described as "a musical mountain spring," and the title appealed to Dr. Caldwell so he adopted the name.

During its heyday, the resort was advertised as one of the most beautiful and attractive locations in the South during the summer months beginning in June and ending in October. A variety of activities welcomed the guests that included swimming and fishing in the local river. Sports such as tennis, bowling, croquet, billiards, and dancing were available for the adults while children enjoyed a separate playground. The resort also advertised the presence of two mineral springs that were represented as having strengthening and curative properties. Unfortunately, the springs dried up following the blasting involved in construction of a new paved road between Valley Head and Mentone in 1928.

Before the depression the hotel was sold several times between 1918 and 1920. This led to deterioration of the facility necessary to accommodate large groups like the Alabama State Baptist Assembly, and the last big church assemblage to meet in Mentone was in 1931. Because of the inability of individuals that leased the hotel to make a profit it eventually closed for several years.

On July 4, 1950, Ben Hammond of Rome, Georgia, purchased the property at an auction to serve as a summer home. It was sold again in 1956 to be used as a home and organ repair shop before closing again for several additional years. The hotel reopened in 2001 and underwent an extensive restoration in 2010-2011.

Like all great hotels, it had its stories of ghosts on the premises to add to the mystical history of the locale. Prior to the fire of March 1, 2014, the hotel was considered "one of the oldest hotels in the State of Alabama" and had been featured in the *New York Times* bestseller *1,000 Places to See Before You Die*.

Before the fire in 2014 the hotel was placed on the National Register of Historical Places. Like many other historical structures in the South, the grand old hotel in Dekalb County deserved a better fate than perishing in the blaze on March 1. However, it can at least be said it avoided the indignity of death by the wrecking ball.

You still have the option of visiting two attractive sites just down from Mentone in either the summer or winter. DeSoto Falls State Park is seven miles from Mentone, and the adjacent DeSoto Falls is one of the tallest and most visited waterfalls in Alabama.

In the winter, Cloudmont Ski and Golf Resort is Alabama's only ski resort and is located on County Road 614, just off the Lookout Mountain Parkway in Mentone. It has excellent facilities for both beginner and intermediate skiers on eight hundred acres on mountain top property.

STEVENSON RAILROAD DEPOT MUSEUM

Stevenson, Alabama, like its nearby neighbor Bridgeport, Alabama, are two small villages that have interesting railroad pasts. Both were important venues before, during and after the Civil War. Unfortunately they both remain sparsely populated today. (However, the towns may like it that way!)

The original Stevenson train depot was built in 1852, and it was destroyed around the Civil War period. During its existence it had a common use by the Nashville and Chattanooga Railroad and by the Memphis and Charleston Railroads with separate tracks for the trains on each side of the depot.

The present depot was built in 1872 and is on the same site as the original one, and it has been suggested that some of the salvaged brick from the original depot has been used in the construction of the second depot.

With the decline of passenger service the tracks on each side of the restored depot still are used for freight trains along the designated routes.

The depot has been converted into the Stevenson Railroad Depot Museum, and it houses a collection of military, agricultural, Indian, railroad, pioneer life artifacts, and other memorabilia. The depot is registered on the National Register of Historic Places.

Possession of the depot changed several times during the Civil War. The Union forces surrounded the railroad junction with blockhouses and an earthen redoubt known as Ford Harker. Its remains are south of the depot.

Fort Harker was constructed by the Union Army in the summer of 1862 and expanded in 1864, using soldiers and freed slaves during the work. Fort Harker was an earthen redoubt, 150 feet square, with walls 14 feet high and surrounded by an 8 foot deep dry powder moat. The fort contained 7 cannon platforms, a bomb-proof powder magazine, a draw bridge entrance, and an 8 sided wooden blockhouse at its center. It is also on the National Register of Historic Places.

Stevenson was a vital link to major points throughout the Southeast, and in 1863 Union General Rosecrans' forces constructed a pontoon bridge across the Tennessee River that year which allowed thousands of Union troops to cross the river and advance on to the battlefield at Chickamauga during the bloody battle held on September 18-20. Historic homes on either end of town were used as Civil War hospitals.

The railroad stop was named for the railroads president Vernon K. Stevenson, who was a close friend of Chattanooga railroad promoter, James A. Whiteside.

While the original objective was to build the railroad from Nashville to Chattanooga, it was also a goal to build the track solely within the State of Tennessee, but the mountainous terrain between the two cities mandated that the railroad had to be re-routed below South Pittsburgh into Alabama. It was also necessary that the Nashville and Chattanooga railroad would go into the State of Georgia for a short distance before going into Chattanooga.

Adjacent to the depot is the Stevenson Hotel that was built simultaneously with the depot. It contained eight rooms with a lobby and two dining rooms that was connected to the depot by a walkway.

The hotel for a long time was the center of cultural activities in Stevenson and was rumored to have been the site of the first showing of a motion picture in the city.

When the railroad abandoned the depot in 1976, a group of local citizens put on a campaign to save the depot. They raised the money to purchase the building and to turn it into the local history museum which exists today.

It, as well as the hotel and 30 more buildings in Stevenson, are also on the National Register of Historical Places. Traditionally the city during the first full week of June each year celebrates the Depot Days Festival which includes a week long event of family oriented activities.

Parker Edmiston is the contact person for the Museum which is located at 207 Main Street at Stevenson, Alabama 35772, phone number (256) 437-3012. Admission is free and the normal hours are Monday through Friday from 8:30 a.m. to 4:30 p.m. (Central Standard Time).

A one day trip to Stevenson, Bridgeport, South Pittsburg, Orme and the Russell Cave National Monument should appeal to the historical appetite and curiosity of all.

The *Depot Days Festival* is traditionally held each June at the Stevenson Railroad Depot Museum

FORT PAYNE, ALABAMA

Fort Payne is located in DeKalb County which is one of three counties carved from the Cherokee Expulsions of 1835. The county was first established on January 9, 1836 at the foot of Lookout Mountain. It was named for Baron DeKalb, who was killed in Camden, South Carolina, during the Revolutionary War. When the Cherokee Indians were removed as part of the treaty of New Echota, stockades and wooden forts were erected for gathering and holding the Indians prior to their removal.

Captain John Payne was sent to the present site of Fort Payne in 1836, and a stockade was built near a large stream. As a result the fort was named in his honor. With the removal of the Indians, settlers began to enter the valley, and by 1840 the county had a population of 5,929. In the next census in 1850, the number of residents had increased to 8,245 in DeKalb County.

Although the county seat was at Lebanon for many years, in 1876 it was moved to Fort Payne. The main reason for the change was the fact that the community was being served by the railroad. Fort Payne was a "boom town" that rapidly grew from a population of 500 to several thousand residents beginning around 1887. That year rumors began to be spread that Fort Payne was surrounded by rich mineral deposits. As a result several speculators began to devise plans for a giant manufacturing city at Fort Payne.

The Fort Payne Coal and Iron Company was organized in 1888 with a capital outlay of $5,000,000 of stock that was sold to the public in New England within five weeks after it was placed on sale. Rapid development took place, with 32,000 acres of land in the area being purchased for the purpose of building a city and in anticipation of the arrival of a large group of investors.

Preparations included road improvements, installation of sewer and water systems, and the rising municipality became known as "The Electric City" after a powerhouse was constructed and electric connections were distributed throughout the community. In February 1889, the City of Fort Payne was incorporated and the growth of the village evolved into the "boom town."

The DeKalb Hotel was built with up-to-date amenities that included rooms lighted with electricity and a dining room with a capacity to serve 150 meals at a time. An opera house was erected and had a grand opening on September 16, 1890, but it fell into disuse and disrepair after the boom growth ended. Its first shown production was Hoyt's "A Tin Soldier." It subsequently became a source for the showing of silent moves around 1918, and the first sound movie was "The Jazz Singer." In 1977 it was listed as the only opera house still in existence in Alabama. A train station was constructed in 1891 and served passengers from October 22, 1891 until August 24, 1970.

Fortunately the opera house and train station have been saved from demolition by having both facilities added to the National Register of Historic Places. During the boom era the city had four banks, several investment companies, an ice company, a clay works making sewer pipes and brick, a stove works, several hardware and lumber companies, a carriage and wagon works and rolling mills. A large advertising campaign by the developers boasted of almost endless deposits of iron ore surrounded the town which caused property values to soar.

Train loads of prospective buyers from New England invaded the area in lavish new parlor cars on the Alabama Great Southern Railroad from Chattanooga to Fort Payne. As a result Southern residents were soon outnumbered by New Englanders. An editorial in one of the town's two newspapers on August 28, 1890 rejected the idea of the land boom becoming a land bust possibility. However in 1891 the land values dropped substantially when it was discovered that the supplies of coal and iron ore near Fort Payne were well below expectations, and there developed a mass exist of the population to Birmingham.

Fort Payne has had several periods of both up and down economic periods. In 1907 the hosiery industry developed into decades of hosiery manufacturing in Fort Payne in over 100 mills employing over 7000 workers and giving it the title of the "Sock Capital of the World."

This likewise suffered a decline when it had to compete with foreign manufacturers from China and elsewhere that caused a reduction in the number of hosiery employees, but the companies diversified from athletic socks to boutique designs to try and stay in business. In the 1990s business and civic leaders led a diversification of the community and brought in other industries.

Located along Interstate 59, it is 53 miles from Chattanooga and 96 miles from Birmingham at exits 218 and 222. In addition to the manufacturing industry, a lucrative tourist industry is being developed in Fort Payne to take advantage of the many natural scenic wonders of the area such a DeSoto Falls State park and Little River Canyon National Preserve.

In 2010 Fort Payne had a population of 14,012 ,which included the county and rock band, Alabama. The band proudly claims it as their home town and houses their fan club and museum there. On the trivia side, in 1989 Fort Payne held the world record for the "Largest Cake Ever Baked" in the *Guinness World Records* when the community jointly produced a 128,238 pound cake to commemorate the city's centennial anniversary.

NOCCALULA FALLS PARK – GADSDEN

The initial inquiry of any reader has to be – who or what was Noccalula? Located on the western end of Lookout Mountain near Gadsden, Alabama is a ninety-foot waterfall. Near the falls is a nine-foot-tall bronze statue of a young Cherokee woman, Noccalula, for whom the falls are named.

Noccalula Falls and sculpture of the Cherokee Indian maiden by the same name

According to an Alabama legend that has been handed down through generations, the maiden was the daughter of a Cherokee chief who lived with his tribe near the waterfall. Noccalula fell in love with a young warrior in her tribe who was a brave man but unfortunately did not possess many worldly goods that would allow him to compete for the maiden's hand as did some of his rivals. Although Noccalula pleaded with her father to approve her chosen warrior he refused to accept him as a future son-in-law and considered him a poor match for his daughter.

Instead the chief arranged for her to marry the wealthy chief of a rival tribe, and he also expelled his daughter's beau from their tribe. As the wedding date approached, people gathered from throughout the region but Noccalula was heartbroken. On her wedding day she was dressed for the event by female relatives, but she could not accept the idea of marrying a man she did not love. She stepped away from the crowd and went to the edge of the waterfall, paused for a moment and then jumped to her death in the swirling water and rocks below to the horror of the onlookers. The father of the young girl realized the harshness of his actions which led to his daughter's suicide and decreed that the waterfall would forever be named for his daughter.

When the tribe was forced to vacate the area and migrate west along the Trail of Tears, the settlers who took over the property maintained the name. As in many of the waterfalls and other places where deaths have occurred, a paranormal legend exists at Noccalula Falls. Some say the young girl can still be seen in its rainbows and mists at the bottom of the waterfall. Another part of the legend is that the ghost of the young maiden still mourns for her true love, and that her ghost appears in the mists and fog at the bottom of the falls on moonlit nights.

Today the falls are surrounded by a popular park and recreation area, and it is one of the most visited attractions in Alabama. Noccalula Falls was listed on the Alabama Register of Landmarks and Heritage on May 12, 1976 and was rated in 2017 as the best campsite in Alabama in a 50-state survey. The entire park sits on a two-hundred-acre public facility.

Other features are a trail winding through Black Creek Gorge at its base. It continues past caves, an aboriginal fort, an abandoned dam, pioneer homestead, and Civil War carvings. Additional amenities include a petting zoo, mini-golf course, a 1899 covered bridge and a replica train ride. Former Gadsden Mayor R. A. Mitchell once owned a part of the property buying 109 acres in 1909. He intended to develop the area into a city park. His daughter sold the property to the city of Gadsden in 1946. Additional acreage was purchased in 1959.

At one time in the second half of the 19th Century, a tavern and dance hall were operated in a cave behind the waterfall but when an attempt was made to enlarge a flat area with dynamite, a cave-in occurred.

To reach Noccalula Falls, travel from Chattanooga on I-24 W to the junction with I-59 and follow Exit 188 to Noccalula Road (Alabama Highway 211). Turn right and travel over the mountain to the waterfall which will be on your right. A foot bridge leads from the parking area to a point where the waterfall can be viewed. The waterfall can be viewed for free. Admission to the pioneer village and park is $6 for adults, $4 for seniors, and $3 for children 4-12. Also on the premises is a wedding chapel near the falls which can accommodate up to 75 guests. For more information call (256) 543-7412.

If you want to get married in a beautiful setting, or just visit a historical and scenic location on a one day trip to Noccalula Falls, it is another attractive location in our area.

RUSSELL CAVE NATIONAL MONUMENT

A short drive from Chattanooga along I-24 W to exit 72 (South Pittsburg) towards Bridgeport, Alabama, leads a traveler to Russell Cave National Monument on the left. It is an archaeological site with one of the most complete records of prehistoric culture of a group of people in the Southeast.

The monument's location in northeastern Alabama is closest to the former railroad town of Bridgeport.

The National Geographical Society donated to the American people 310 acres which encompasses the area of the cave. The Society had previously purchased the site in 1956 from Oscar Ridley. With this donation the monument is now administered and maintained by the National Park Service.

The original owner of the property was Major James Dorian who was the brother-in-law of Colonel Thomas Russell, a veteran of the American Revolutionary War from North Carolina and for whom the cave is named.

Starting in 1953 the Chattanooga chapter of the Tennessee Archaeological Society first excavated and recognized Russell Cave as an archaeological site. The National Geographical Society as well as the Smithsonian Institute conducted additional excavations along with the National Park Service.

After the property had been donated to the United States government in 1961, President John F. Kennedy proclaimed Russell Cave a National Monument on May 11 of that year.

The excavation work is ongoing, and to date the teams have dug down more than 30 feet into the cave floor.

Using carbon-14 testing to determine the ages of ancient campfire residue found, the teams have been able to surmise the age of these artifacts as being about 6500 years. However the ages of human remains also found suggest a much older date of occupation of possibly 10,000 years.

The cave is believed to have primarily been used as a seasonal winter shelter based on the ability of the settlers to rely on the surrounding forest area to grow produce and to hunt for game and fish in surrounding water sources of the Tennessee River.

Russell Cave is the third-longest mapped cave in the State of Alabama and is ranked 90th on the United States Long Cave list and 314 on the World Long Cave List.

Russell Cave continues to be an extremely important archaeological research site but has also become a popular tourist destination. The Grosvenor Visitor Center, which was dedicated in 1967, contains museum exhibits and documentary films about the lifestyles of prehistoric peoples. The center was named after Gilbert H. Grosvenor who was the editor of the *National Geographic Society Magazine* from 1903 to 1954 and president of the National Geographical Society from 1920-1954.

Recreational caving is no longer available, but tours led by Park Rangers are free and there are two walking trails. Russell Cave is one of the most extensive cave systems in Alabama with more than seven miles of mapped passageways. It also contains five separate entrances into the cave.

A rare specimen of a scorpion that has not been found anywhere else in the world has been found in the cave and is protected.

Each year during the first weekend in May the Russell Cave National Monument has hosted a Native American Festival. The event includes Indian performances, and the reenactment of a Cherokee encampment is conducted. A variety of demonstrations are held in wood carving, and pottery hand building.

Easily located at 3729 County Road 98 outside Bridgeport, the cave site is open year around, and admission is free to enter the park or tour the cave.

A call to the monument office at (256)-495-2672 will connect you with courteous staff members who can provide you with up-to-date information about the site.

If you want to make it an all day trip you can also continue up 98 until you see a sign on the right that will direct you to the abandoned railroad depot in the former mining town of Orme, Tennessee, that is in Marion County, Tennessee.

LOST TOWNS OF ALABAMA
WATERLOO & RIVERTON

The control of the often-raging Tennessee, Ohio, and other rivers by the erection of hydroelectric dams in the Tennessee Valley brought many benefits to the communities and residents of several states.

However, with all government projects, there are always negative aspects that have to be weighed against the ultimate good results.

There is no doubt that the Tennessee Valley Authority's (TVA) multiple hydroelectric dams transformed the Tennessee Valley and has made life easier for its residents. For some several thousand homeowners and tenant farmers, though, the unified plan meant sacrificing home and community for the public good.

Two small towns in particular, Waterloo and Riverton in Alabama, would pay the highest price of the creation of the dam system and particularly the vast reservoir and Pickwick Landing Dam. Hamilton County also lost a couple of islands when the spillways of the Chickamauga Dam were closed on January 15, 1940. Chickamauga Island was located just upstream of the dam and was quickly submerged. The waters of the lake did not cover Dallas Island until nearly three months later.

When President Franklin Delano Roosevelt signed the original Tennessee Valley Act on May 18, 1933 as part of his New Deal legislation designed to attempt to bring the country out of the Great Depression, several positive and negative consequences for the citizens of the two Alabama towns took place.

The communities of Waterloo and Riverton existed prior to the construction of Pickwick Dam and were dependent on agricultural income derived from lands that would be included in the vast reservoir.

The dam system that began at the junction of the Holston and French Broad Rivers in Tennessee would eventually cover approximately eight hundred eighty-six miles of navigable water ways in a

U-shaped course, and twenty-nine hydroelectric dams, with the first sixteen dams being completed and put in service in eleven years.

The goals of the system were to (1) reduce flooding; (2) provide a navigable waterway; (3) generate electric power; and (4) provide clean and safe waterways to eliminate hazardous areas such as "the Suck" in Hamilton County, and a portion of the treacherous Muscle Shoals in Alabama.

The vast reservoir created by the Pickwick Landing Dam would affect parts of counties in Tennessee, Mississippi and Alabama that would be submerged.

The initial euphoria was to transform the vast multi-state region by providing good paying jobs when TVA recruited many workers from the agricultural population to clear the land and to work on the construction of the dam.

Due to the dam being built, eventually five hundred six families were relocated and cemeteries, highways, bridges and utility lines were either moved or protected. Because of the economic benefit of the available good paying jobs the crisis of community readjustment was deferred. It was erroneously believed that the dislocated persons would move out of the area, but the personal attachment to their former homeland would result in them staying close to the family roots.

After the dam was finished, employment opportunities in the area became scarce because the communities of Waterloo and Riverton and its residents were primarily farmers who were dependent on agricultural income from land that would be included in the reservoir area to be flooded.

Initially some Riverton residents would continue to find jobs on the Colbert Shoals Canal Lock which was first named Riverton Lock. Colbert and Bee Tree Shoals were upriver from Riverton and prevented major river traffic between Riverton and Florence, Alabama for six months of the dry season. After Muscle Shoals Canal Lock was started, the task of overseeing the completion of the lock was assigned to a captain in the Army Corps of Engineers, George Washington Goethals, who later would be promoted to general and was given the responsibility of designing and constructing the Panama Canal.

With the completion of the Muscle Shoals Canal Lock the displaced Riverton residents once again faced unemployment.

The former inhabitants of Waterloo did not fare much better as they initially received some support from the lumber business, but it was estimated that all marketable lumber from the area of the submerged twin towns and the reservoirs would be cut within two or three years.

The debate on the benefits of providing flood control, navigation and electricity to the region versus the loss of property and the sacrifice of the towns of Waterloo and Riverton extended even to the naming of Pickwick Dam.

The designation of the area using the name Pickwick Landing Dam came from the location of the dam near Pickwick Landing which had derived its name from the local post office. The area's first postmaster was fond of Charles Dickens novel *The Pickwick Papers* and honored the author by naming his post office after him.

As expected, controversy arose when some political supporters wanted to name the dam after either Tennessee Senator Kenneth McKellar or Mississippi Congressman John Elliott Rankin. Civil War historians advocated for the facility to be renamed to honor the Battle of Shiloh. Eventually all other proposals failed, and the name Pickwick Landing Dam remained.

Today it would have to be recognized that the sacrifice of the Alabama towns of Waterloo and Riverton were for the greater good and was a beneficial price for progress.

HOTEL TUTWILER – BIRMINGHAM

The first modern hotel in Birmingham (The Magic City) was built in 1914 by two prominent businessmen, Robert Jemison, Jr. and George Crawford Major Tutwiler, who was the main financial supporter through his Tutwiler Coal and Coke Company.

The hotel was originally built in order to convince the American Iron and Steel Institute to have its annual convention in Birmingham. At the time it was erected there were no other luxury hotel accommodations, and the Tutwiler would be considered one of the finest hotels in the country. Today a portion of it remains but at a different location. Originally the hotel was built on the corner of 20th Street and 5th Avenue North in downtown Birmingham.

Like all luxury hotels of the time, it had a spectacular era of galas, famous guests and historical events. Several high-profile events such as Tallulah Bankhead's post wedding party, and a press conference held by Charles Lindbergh on his nationwide tour with the Spirit of St. Louis to promote aviation after his Atlantic crossing from New Jersey to Paris in 1927.

Unfortunately like many other grand hotels of the era that have been razed, the Tutwiler also slowly deteriorated to the point where it was closed and faced demolition. In 1974 it finally reached the point where the original hotel was imploded.

After a twelve-year absence, the name Hotel Tutwiler rose like a phoenix out of its ashes and took over the Ridgely Apartments a few blocks away on Park Place, thus reinstating the name Hotel Tutwiler from its downtown landscape after an absence of twelve years.

In 1985 the City of Birmingham was awarded an Urban Development Act grant, and with some private financing, the old hotel was reopened. The original marble floors, exterior and vaulted railings were maintained in its renovation. Many modern amenities such as a fitness center, business center, signature restaurant and suites have been added. Only a swimming pool is missing but the hotel's history of offering rooms with a view was included, as all of the 149 rooms feature expansive windows that show off the city scope of the modern Birmingham.

Like all grand luxury hotels of the past, the Tutwiler has its stories of its resident "ghost." The hotel's story is that Major Tutwiler, who formerly lived at the Ridgely Apartments, decided to stay at the new Hotel Tutwiler, and that his spirit, known as "The Knocker," has the bad habit of knocking on doors at late hours. Other tales claim he sometimes causes havoc in the bar and restaurant.

One story goes that a bartender got in trouble because he allegedly left the lights and stoves on after closing hours for several nights. The manager came in early one morning to discover that someone had prepared a large meal and drunk a bottle of wine. Thus, developed its tradition of the staff addressing the ghost of Major Tutwiler with the words "Goodnight Major" and asking him not to mess up the kitchen.

The hotel is now officially the Hampton Inn & Suites Downtown Tutwiler Birmingham. It is located at 2021 Park Place, Birmingham, Alabama 35203.

Centrally located and reasonably priced, a stay at the Tutwiler gives a visitor an enjoyable historical trip to the past era if you don't meet the ghost of Major Tutwiler or hear from "The Knocker."

COON DOG CEMETERY
CHEROKEE, ALABAMA

The purpose of this article is not to require a hunter to make a choice as to whether he should provide the most expensive funeral for his believed coon dog or his faithful wife.

The Coon Dog Cemetery is located 7 miles west of Tuscumbia, Alabama in Colbert County on U.S. 72 near Cherokee, Alabama. Turn off the highway onto Alabama 247 and travel approximately 12 miles before turning right onto Coon Dog Cemetery Road and follow the signs.

Eighty-three years ago a hunter by the name of Key Underwood buried his dog, a coonhound named Troop, in an old hunting camp where the two of them had enjoyed coon hunting for years. As a result other hunters also buried their favorite coon dogs there. They erected appropriate headstones in the animal's name and often with other epitaphs such as "He wasn't the best, but he was the best I ever owned!"

Thus the cemetery came into being and today is run by a five member Board of Friends of Coon Dog Cemetery. Of these only two are coon hunters, cousins Lee Hatton and Frank Hatton.

Dogs must meet three stringent requirements to qualify for burial in the cemetery: (1) the owner must certify that this dog is a purebred coonhound; (2) a witness must declare that the deceased is a coon dog that has been hunted; and (3) a member of the local coon hunters organization must be allowed to view the coonhound's body and certify it to be a purebred.

One restriction is that mixed breed or pet dogs are not allowed to be buried in the graveyard. A one-time perpetual care fee of $100 is due prior to burial, and at least one photograph of the coon dog must be provided to the Board.

The headstones range from basic wood and metal monuments up to elaborate marble engraved stones similar to ones found in upscale human cemeteries. Supporters claim that it is the only cemetery in the world specifically dedicated to the preservation of the memory of coonhounds.

The cemetery was inaugurated on Labor Day in 1937, so on that date every year a large celebration is held with blue grass music, buck dancing, barbecue and a liar's contest.

A monument in Coon Dog Cemetery

Admission is free to the public, but donations are accepted to meet the $234.00 monthly upkeep fee. Hats and t-shirts with the Coon Dog Cemetery logo are available for purchase, and raffle items are auctioned off to raise additional up-keep funds.

Belt buckles with coon dog designs and coonskin caps similar to those worn by Davy Crockett and Tennessee Senator Estes Kefauver in his political campaigns are available for purchase. Each grave site is decorated with an American flag as a gesture honoring the deceased. Politicians are often in attendance but no active politicking is allowed.

The cemetery has grown to be the final honored resting place for over approximately 400 coon dogs.

The hallowed ground has been memorialized in a song by Travis Wammack titled "Coon Dog Cemetery" and the cemetery was featured in the movie, *Sweet Home Alabama*.

Loyalties and feelings run high in the coonhound community. One long-time coon hunter once had a wife. She felt like the long nights away from home by her husband tracking coons had gotten out of hand. Finally, she told him, "It's either me or the dogs."

After the divorce the dog owner became engaged to a lovely lady who accepted her fiancés love of his coon dogs and their relationship became quite content.

Although the Labor Day celebration for 2020 had to be canceled because of the corona-virus epidemic, plans for the 2021 event are already in the works.

Mark your calendar for 2021 to take a trip to the only coon dog cemetery in existence. (Don't forget to bring your lawn chairs.)

JOHN HEISMAN – FOOTBALL INNOVATOR (1869-1936)

Most sports fans can quickly identify John Heisman as the name on the trophy awarded to the most outstanding collegiate football player in America each year. However, only the really dedicated sports fans are familiar with his extensive coaching career at eight major universities and his multi-faceted career as a basketball and baseball coach, athletic director, creator of the forward pass, sports writer, actor, law student, and head of the New York Downtown Athletic Club. He was also famously associated with educational institutions in Alabama and Georgia.

John Heisman was born on October 23, 1869, in Cleveland, Ohio, and attended Brown University and the University of Pennsylvania where he gained his law degree. During his playing career he played center, tackle, and end as a 158-pound lineman. In his early career at Oberlin College and Buchtel, Heisman became an innovator and produced many changes on the football field. He was responsible for implementing the "flying wedge" offense which consisted of seven players in the form of a "V" protecting the runner. Due to numerous injuries taking place with the tactic it was declared illegal to use in a game.

Heisman is also credited with developing the forward pass and turning football into "a game of science." Temporarily Heisman was out of coaching and was working at a tomato farm in Marshall, Texas. When the manager, Walter Riggs of the Alabama Polytechnic Institute (Auburn University) contacted Heisman and offered him the position of being head football coach for the large sum of $500, John headed for the Plains of Auburn.

During the years 1895-1899 Heisman revolutionized the football program at Auburn. The school's yearbook praised Heisman and described his arrival at the school "as the luckiest in the history of athletics at the Auburn Polytechnic Institute."

He continued to develop new tactics including using oral commands such as "hike" or "hut" directing the center to put the ball in play. This often led to the opposing team jumping offsides and receiving a penalty. Heisman was a vocal coach both at practice and in the game and would constantly urge and demand that his players put forth their maximum effort.

Other new tactics were the "hidden ball trick" that is occasionally still used today. He also was one of the main proponents of making the forward pass legal after he saw it used in a game between the University of North Carolina and Auburn University in 1895.

The year 1896 is best remembered for two off the field stunts. Auburn players greased the tracks that carried the Georgia Tech team to Auburn and the train could not be stopped until it went five miles past the Auburn Depot. The Tech players had to walk back to Auburn and lost 45-0 to the Tigers. Many claimed that the long walk was a significant contributing factor. As a result of the lopsided victory another tradition was started – the student body proceeding through the streets of Auburn in their pajamas, known as the "Wreck Tech Pajama Parade."

In 1897 Auburn traveled to the University of the South at Sewanee and engaged in a scoreless tie with the little Episcopal school. Because of a debt of $700 incurred during the football season, Heisman used his acting experience from early in life and produced and staged a comedy play at Auburn titled *David Garrick*. This was just one of many performances by Heisman in several acting troupes in the off season. He was known for using his acting talents to motivate and inspire his players. With the proceeds of the play Auburn was able to field another team in 1898.

The year 1898 produced what Heisman described as his best team at Auburn. Heisman initiated what today is a common part of both college and professional football – the hurry up offense. Heisman over the years would continue to use new and unknown tactics that would often not only confuse the opposing team but also the officials calling the game.

The 1899 team lost only one game 11-10 to the "Iron Men" of Sewanee, who shut out all of their other opponents. Heisman left Auburn after the 1899 season and spent four seasons at Clemson (1900-1903), fifteen seasons at Georgia Tech (1904-1919), three seasons at Pennsylvania (1920-1923), and four seasons at Rice (1924-1927). In 1927 Heisman retired to lead the Downtown Athletic Club in New York and in 1935 it began awarding what is now known at the Heisman Trophy.

John Heisman died on October 3, 1936, in New York City of pneumonia and was buried in his wife's hometown of Rhinelander, Wisconsin. He was inducted into the second class of the College Football Hall of Fame in 1954 as a coach.

HELEN KELLER – A COMPLEX LIFE STORY

The life of Helen Keller is one of the most admired and controversial stories of an individual overcoming the dual handicaps of being both deaf and blind at the same time. She has been an inspiration to unknown numbers of individuals with similar or other physical or mental afflictions.

The production *The Miracle Worker* is a 1962 American biographical film about Anne Sullivan's bond to Helen Keller and starring Anne Bancroft and Patty Duke as the principal actresses. The film won five Academy Awards with Bancroft receiving the Best Actress Award and Duke the Best Supporting Actress Award.

The off Broadway play of the story took place in June – July 2020 for the 59th season in the Alabama town of Tuscumbia, located approximately 170 miles from Chattanooga on U.S. Highway 72 W past Huntsville and Decatur in Colbert County. It is about 20 miles East of the Natchez Trace Parkway.

Her birthplace, Ivy Green, a Southern plantation, was built in 1820 and was made a permanent shrine and placed on the National Register of Historic Places in 1954. Adjacent to the main house is Helen's birthplace cottage and consists of a large room with a lovely bay window and playroom. The structures contain the Keller families' original furnishings, hundreds of personal mementos, gifts and books from a lifetime of travels in thirty-nine countries on five different continents.

It is located at 300 N. Commons St. W, Tuscumbia, Alabama 35674 (256) 383-4066. Admission is charged to tour the facility.

Helen Adams Keller was born a healthy child on June 27, 1880 to Captain Arthur H. and Kate Adams Keller of Tuscumbia. He father was an officer in the Confederate Army during the Civil War and was an editor of the Tuscumbia North Alabamian newspaper for many years. Her mother was also the daughter of a Confederate general.

At the age of 19 months, Helen contracted an unknown illness described by some physicians as similar to scarlet fever or meningitis. As a result, she became both deaf and blind. She was a wild and belligerent child coping with her dual handicaps and at the age of six was taken to an appointment with Dr. Alexander Graham Bell by her parents at his "School of Vocal Physiology and Mechanics for Speech" in Boston.

The visit resulted with the unruly child meeting Anne Mansfield Sullivan as her teacher on March 3, 1887. Eventually Helen would learn the fingertip alphabet and then learn to write. In six months, she knew 625 words to communicate with Anne Sullivan.

By the age of ten Helen had mastered Braille and the manual alphabet and could operate a typewriter.

With self-determination she learned to speak by the age of 16 well enough to attend preparatory school, and in 1904 she graduated *cum laude* from Radcliffe College as a Phi Beta Kappa Scholar.

In 1903 while still a student, she wrote *The Story of My Life."*

During her life she learned five languages in Braille, wrote eleven books and numerous articles and lectured in thirty more countries on five continents.

She also received the Presidential Medal of Freedom, the highest honor an American citizen can receive, from President Lyndon B. Johnson for political activism.

On her 100th birthday, President Jimmy Carter in 1980

Helen Keller of Tuscumbia, Alabama

posthumously issued a presidential proclamation to recognize her accomplishments.

Her remarkable life was not without some controversy during this era, as she was a prolific author, political activist and socialist. Always outspoken in her convictions, she became a member of the Socialist Party of America and actively campaigned and wrote articles in support of the working class.

Keller spoke in twenty-five countries about the problems of deaf persons and the conditions under which they had to live.

She was both admired and disliked for her various roles as a women's suffragist, pacifist, radical socialist, birth control supporter and opponent of President Woodrow Wilson. Her liberal stands on behalf of the NAACP, and as a founder of the ACLU resulted in some censorship of her writings by the Rockefeller National Newspaper chain, but she fought back, and they relented and her words were again published.

The attitude of some columnists changed from praise and admiration for her work on behalf of the deaf and blind before she expressed her socialist point of view. Instead they criticized her viewpoints on the basis of her disabilities as being the cause of her liberal stands on social issues.

She defended her motivation for disagreement by stating that it came in part from her "concern about blindness and other disabilities."

The complexity of Helen Keller's life is too enormous to be covered in a short article. Readers are respectfully urged to Google her name and review the numerous sources that describe in great detail how this remarkable woman demonstrated how her dual handicaps did not prevent her from living a full (and controversial) life.

In 1961 she suffered a series of strokes that resulted in her being homebound in her home "Arcan Ridge" in Easton, Connecticut. She devoted much of her later life to raising funds for the American Federation for the Blind.

She died in her sleep on June 1, 1968 a few weeks short of her eighty-eight birthday and her ashes are buried at the Washington

National Cathedral in Washington, D.C., beside her two constant teachers and companions, Anne Sullivan and Polly Thompson.

American has never had a more accomplished (and controversial) individual who overcame her severe handicaps than Helen Keller!

PAT TRAMMELL – SCOTTSBORO AND BAMA'S ALL AMERICAN

The first time that Chattanooga's athletes became aware of Patrick Lee Trammell was when his Scottsboro Wildcats were invited to participate in the annual preseason Times Cup basketball tournament at the John B. Steele Gymnasium at City High School on 3rd Street in December 1956. After beating Chattanooga's Central Purple Pounders, by a score of 67-66 in the semi-finals, his Scottsboro team would meet City High in the finals of the tournament.

In 1957 Trammell would lead the Wildcats against the eventual Tennessee State Football Champions Central High Purple Pounders in a 26-12 loss in Scottsboro.

The annual Scottsboro Invitational held during the week after Christmas in 1957 would include another basketball encounter between Central and Scottsboro. Although Scottsboro and Central had been the pre-tournament favorites, they had been upset in the second round by DAR and New Hope and would meet in the consolation round. Central would prevail 65-55, although Trammell led the scoring for Scottsboro with 27 points outscoring Central's Eddie Test by five points.

Trammell would be selected as the Most Valuable Basketball Player in the State of Alabama for 1958 and would earn All Country, All State, All Southern, and All American honors during the 1958 season as the leader of the Wildcat football squad.

The relationship between Pat Trammell and legendary college football coach Paul "Bear" Bryant is part of the resurrection of football history of Alabama football. Although Pat had originally planned to sign with Georgia Tech after his senior year in 1958, Coach Bryant promised to come coach at Alabama, his alma mater, and leave Texas A&M if Pat would commit to Alabama.

Thus started a lifelong relationship with Bryant that led to the supreme compliment in his autobiography, *Bear*, about Pat Trammell when he stated that the day Pat died was "the saddest day of my life."

On the day of Pat's funeral in Scottsboro, Coach Bryant was seen crying for the only recognized time in his lengthy life and career when he escorted Pat's mother out of the Church.

Although Coach Bryant had several "favorite" players during his career he expressed in a sentimental moment, "Pat Trammell was [not just my favorite player but] the favorite person…of my entire life."

Patrick Lee Trammell

Pat was also one of the few players who could argue with Coach Bryant and even reject plays sent in by him from the sidelines.

Pat Trammell came from a family of physicians and declined an inquiry from Green Bay's Coach Vince Lombardi about playing for the Packers in the National Football League if they could draft Pat. He expressed early on that his goal in life was to be a doctor, and he accomplished that by becoming a dermatologist as a third generation doctor in 1966 when he graduated from the Medical College of Alabama.

As a treating physician he received another superb compliment when Auburn football Coach Ralph "Shug" Jordan chose Pat to treat his skin cancer. Jordan would also attend Pat's funeral.

Pat died of complications from metastatic testicular cancer on December 10, 1968 at the age of 28 which was only two years after earning his M.D. degree. He left a wife and two small children. His legacy has lived on since his death. From 1968-2014 numerous accounts of his life, establishment of scholarships, and creation of many programs that benefit young people have been set up in his name.

The awards and honors that Pat Trammell received during his life and after his death are too numerous to list in a short article.

The readers are respectfully suggested to Google "Patrick Lee 'Pat' Trammell Alabama Football" to ascertain the honors he received but more importantly to realize the respect that this young man achieved in his short life from his community, state and nation.

Those of us who had the privilege to play against Pat Trammell in football and basketball in 1957-1958 did not realize the extent of his ability to lead others and the influence that is still recognized by Alabama and elsewhere. We now do.

DAVID McCAMPBELL – ALABAMA AIR ACE (1910-1996)

As a native of Bessemer, Alabama, David McCampbell was the United States Navy's all-time leading flying ace and the top F6F Hellcat ace with 34 aerial victories over Japanese aircraft in the Pacific during 1944 in World War II.

After short stints at Staunton Military Academy in Staunton, Virginia, and one year at George Tech in Atlanta, Georgia, McCampbell received an appointment to the United States Naval Academy and graduated in 1933 with a degree in marine engineering.

He would receive his "flying wings" on April 21, 1938 at Naval Air Station, Pensacola, Florida, and was originally assigned to the aircraft carrier, USS Ranger in May 1940 as a landing signal officer (LSO) from that date on various ships.

He survived the sinking of the aircraft carrier, USS Wasp by a Japanese submarine near Guadalcanal on September 15, 1942.

Returning to the United States he rose in rank to Lieutenant Commander and was stationed at Naval Air Station Melbourne, Florida, where he served as LSO instructor until August 1943.

McCampbell's heroic actions which led him to be awarded the Medal of Honor from President Franklin Roosevelt took place in 1944 beginning on June 11 when he made his first kill of a Mitsubishi AGM Zeke (Zero) near Saipan in the Marians Islands. From that date through November 14, 1944 he shot down 34 enemy aircraft.

As Commander of Air Group 15 (AG15) from February 1944 to November 1944 he was air commander of the USS Essex aircraft carrier assemblage of fighters, bombers and torpedo bombers. The unit participated in the First and Second Battles of the Philippine Sea. Air Group 15, titled the "Fabled Fifteen," destroyed more enemy planes (315 in the air and 348 on the ground) and sank more enemy shipping than any other unit in the Pacific War.

US Navy Air David McCampbell

Individually McCampbell became the Navy's "ace of aces" for his record in 1944.

Although often outnumbered by enemy fighters, the AG 15 achieved an outstanding record.

Two significant dates are important in McCampbell's resumé against the enemy.

On June 19, 1944 during the fabled "Mariana Turkey Shoot" he shot down five Japanese 'Judy' dive bombers to earn his classification as an "ace" pilot. He re-fueled and later that day shot down two more Japanese "Zekes" over the island of Guam.

However this was not his most outstanding achievement as a fighter pilot. On October 24, 1944 during the Battle of Leyte Gulf, he destroyed a total of nine enemy planes including 7 Zeros and 2 "Oscars." Ironically when he landed his Grumman F6F Hellcat on the USS Langley, his six machine guns had just two rounds remaining and he was out of fuel.

His last destruction of an enemy aircraft took place on November 14, 1944 in Manila Bay in the Philippines when he shot down an "Oscar" to finalize his total of 34 kills.

Following World War II McCampbell served in many capacities in the naval command structure during peacetime and in Korea as well as commands on several ships including the aircraft carrier USS Bon Homme Richard.

He would be awarded the Medal of Honor by Franklin D. Roosevelt prior to the president's death on April 12, 1945. McCampbell would be awarded numerous other recognitions including the Navy Cross, the Silver Star, and Distinguished Flying Cross.

McCampbell retired from active duty in 1964 after 31 years of service. He would live out his retirement in the State of Florida at Rivera Beach and would die on June 30, 1996 at the age of 86. He was interred in Arlington National Cemetery.

He is one of over thirty military personnel from the State of Alabama who were awarded the Medal of Honor through the Vietnam War.

HOWELL HEFLIN – JUSTICE AND SENATOR

Politics was a tradition of the Heflin name in Alabama. Howell Heflin was a nephew of James Thomas Heflin, a well-known white supremacist in the state, who also served as a United States Senator. He was also great nephew of Robert Stell Heflin who served in the House of Representatives in Congress. Howell Heflin was born in Poulan in Worth County, Georgia, on June 19, 1921. He attended the Alabama public schools and graduated from Birmingham Southern College in 1942.

In World War II he served in the United States Marine Corps from 1942-1946 as an officer and distinguished himself as a soldier at the invasions of Bougainville and Guam winning the Silver Star medal and two Purple Hearts for being wounded. Upon returning from military service he went to law school at the University of Alabama graduating in 1948. He established a law practice in Tuscumbia, Alabama and also served as a law professor at Tuscaloosa for twenty years.

Unlike many politicians Heflin was an active and accomplished trial lawyer. In that capacity he was held in high esteem by his fellow attorneys and selected for membership in the International Academy of Trial Lawyers, American College of Trial Lawyers, and the International Society of Barristers, based on legal talent and ethics. He was selected as Chief Justice of the Alabama Supreme Court in 1971 and served until 1977. During that term of service he is credited with reforming the Alabama antiquated court system by improving efficiency and getting the Judicial Article of 1973 enacted by the Alabama legislature. This was a major revision of the state's outmoded 1901 constitution.

When he retired from the court in 1977 the state's court system was considered to be a national model. In 1978 he was elected to the United States Senate. He became a powerful committee chairman as well as a strong advocate for southern agriculture, judicial reform and economic development for the State of Alabama.

He had succeeded John Sparkman, who had been Adlai E. Stevenson's running mate in the 1952 presidential race. He was the last popularly elected Democrat from Alabama although his colleague Richard Shelby had been elected as a Democrat but later switched to the Republican Party.

While in the Senate, Heflin in March 1981 was greatly affected by the shooting of President Ronald Reagan by John Hinckley and the fact that his case was not brought to trial until fourteen months had passed from the date of the incident. He advocated for the need for an overhaul of the criminal system to deal with what he described as a "rising epidemic of violent crime in the nation." He further spoke in favor of putting aside petty partisan politics and uniting both parties in an effort to wage a successful war on crime.

Heflin was a conservative Democrat who strongly opposed gun control and abortion, supported prayer in schools, and opposed laws banning discrimination on the basis of sexual orientation. As a military veteran of WWII he supported the Gulf War of 1991 and opposed cuts in military spending and on occasion voted with the Senate Republicans on tax reform.

He and his colleague Senator Fritz Hollins of South Carolina were the only Democrats to vote against the Family and Medical Leave Act. In 1984 and 1990 he successfully won second and third terms in the Senate but chose not to seek a fourth term in 1996.

Although his family and political background was clothed in segregation, he in 1993 made a memorable speech in support of an effort to deny renewal of a Confederate Flag design for the United Daughters of the Confederacy in spite of his love and pride of his Confederate ancestors.

Heflin died of a heart attack on March 29, 2005 in his hometown of Tuscumbia but not before he anonymously made a gift of $1 million dollars to the University of Alabama Law School for scholarships for deserving young people. Numerous honors and public recognitions were made in his name and the *New York Times* described Heflin as the "conscience of the Senate."

Senator Heflin is often remembered today as a model of public service to Alabama, as a man who obtained great power and applied that power for the common good.

BIG JIM FOLSOM – ALABAMA'S UNIQUE GOVERNOR – No. 1

James Elisha Folsom, Sr. was born on October 9, 1908, and was one of the most colorful of the non-conventional politicians in the State of Alabama in the 1940's-1970's era.

In the era of segregation in the South, he was a rare southern governor who supported a position of moderation on integration and improving the civil rights of blacks. Standing at 6'8" and weighing 250 pounds he early on acquired the nickname "Big Jim Folsom" and in his first campaign for governor in 1946 he used the motto of "the little man's big friend." His only prior successful political experience was as a delegate to the 1944 Democratic National Convention where he opposed the replacement of Vice President Henry Wallace on the Franklin Roosevelt ticket with Harry S. Truman.

Folsom was first elected governor in 1946. His colorful campaign included a hillbilly band, the Strawberry Pickers, that entertained the crowds that came to hear him speak on the issues. Hank Williams, Jr. had briefly been a member of the band. Another of his props was a mop and bucket that he brandished and promised to "clean out the Capitol in Montgomery."

Folsom's first term in office was not without controversy. Rumor of promiscuity and corruption became charges that did not adversely hamper his appeal to the electorate as his first wife Sarah Carnley Folsom, who bore him two daughters, had died in 1944 and he was a bachelor until he married Janelle Moore, a twenty year old secretary at the state highway department on May 5, 1948. She bore him seven children until her death in 1987.

Two months before, a thirty-year-old cashier at the Tutwiler Hotel in Birmingham, Christine Johnson, filed a paternity suit against Big Jim claiming he was the father of her twenty-two month old son. The suit was later dropped pursuant to a cash settlement and in later years Big Jim acknowledged in an interview that he was the father of the child.

Despite rumors of corruption, Folsom was elected governor in the 1954 campaign after sitting out the 1950 race because of the now repealed provision in the Alabama constitution that a governor could not succeed himself in office.

George C. Wallace had been a protégé of Big Jim. He would eventually marry Cornelia Ellis Snevely Folsom, daughter of Jim's sister Ruby Folsom, who was with Wallace when he was badly injured in an assassination attempt on Laurel, Maryland, in 1972. Wallace would run against Folsom in the 1962 Alabama race on a segregation platform. One of the main accusations against Big Jim was his taking of graft. Wallace used the slogan "Something for everybody and a little bit for Big Jim."

Folsom addressed the issue head on and on one occasion told a campaign crowd, "I plead guilty to stealing, That crowd I got it from, you had to steal it to get it. …I stole it for you."

Political supporters still contend that Big Jim would still have won the election except that he appeared intoxicated on a statewide television appearance. Although he kept the progressive integration and black vote, he was defeated by the image-conscious middle class electorate. Folsom contended he had been drugged, but the damage had been done, and he was defeated.

Big Jim ran again for governor in 1966 but lost in a crowded democratic primary to Governor George Wallace's first wife, Lurleen Burns Wallace, who ran as a surrogate candidate because of the antiquated Alabama non-succession constitutional provision.

The former giant later ran several times for public office but was never again considered a serious candidate. Legally blind, he fought with his enemies in the Alabama legislature who first revoked his pension as governor but had it restored in a smaller amount by Republican governor Fob James (Baylor School graduate) that also provided him with a state car and chauffeur.

Big Jim Folsom died on November 21, 1987, in Cullman, Alabama, at the age of seventy-nine thus ending the career of one of Alabama's most colorful and controversial governors.

BIG JIM FOLSOM – NO. 2

One of the best sources of ideas for my articles has come from readers around the Tri-State area who have sent me additional information about the persons and topics in the original writing. Such is the case following the October 14, 2019, article on Alabama's controversial governor, "Big Jim" Folsom.

In 1947 Chattanooga Central was the defending Tennessee High School State Championship football team from 1946. Birmingham Ensley was the Alabama champ during that same year.

Legendary Central and later Baylor coach, E.B. "Red" Etter and likewise legendary Central line coach, Stanley J. Farmer, contacted the Ensley coach and scheduled a game to be played in Birmingham during the 1947 season.

Prior to the game both squads were invited to Governor Folsom's residence in Montgomery for dinner. The story as told by Central All-City guard J.T. Vick was that the team went to the dining room, took their seats and both coaches made some opening remarks.

Big Jim stood up, talked for a while, then announced he was hungry and requested the waiter staff to bring in the food. The staff started bringing in what were described as the biggest T-Bone steaks that most players had ever seen, and starting placing them on trays in the middle of the table. Each player also had a complimentary bottle of whiskey placed beside their plates. Big Jim wrapped a napkin around his neck, grabbed the first steak and told everyone to "dig in" and began eating the steak with his hands and drinking straight from the bottle.

Coach Etter was mortified, Coach Farmer was laughing, and all of the players did like Big Jim and ate the steaks with their hands. Coach Etter made certain no one got into the whiskey.

The game was the next day, and it had rained all night, and the field was muddy. Both teams had been jawing at each other over the two days. On the first play a fight took place between the two teams. It started between Central Captain, Lamar Wheat, who played tackle from Central and James Ivey of Ensley, the other team Captain who also played tackle. When they got to the line on the first play, J.T. Vick threw a handful of mud in Ivey's face. Ivey thought Lamar had done it, and they all got into a muddy fistfight on the field. Both Lamar and the other Captain were ejected from the game.

Central had a chance to score before the half, but time ran out when they were on the one yard line. The game ended in a 0-0 tie.

Lamar Wheat went to Georgia Tech and was an All-American player. He also was inducted into the initial Central Sports Hall of Fame in 2013.

BIG RUBY OF ALABAMA

When you are the sister of ex-Governor James Elisha "Big Jim" Folsom and the mother of Cornelia Wallace, second wife of George C. Wallace, three time governor of Alabama and unsuccessful candidate for President of the United States, you have to be a big part of the history of the State of Alabama.

Ruby Lee Folsom Ellis Austin was a bigger than life character in the colorful and often corrupt state government in Montgomery. "Big Ruby" (she was over six foot tall) was born on May 27, 1913 in Elba, Alabama and died on April fool's Day in 2000 at Enterprise, Alabama. She was five years younger than Big Jim whose populist campaign led him to the governorship in Alabama in 1947-1951 and 1955-1959.

Big Jim was a widower during his first term of office and "Big Ruby" was the First Lady of Alabama while her brother was Governor during his second term. The stories about her are almost as zany as those of her older brother.

After George Wallace married Ruby's daughter Cornelia in 1971, her home became kind of an open house for hangers on to come in and get something to eat or drink.

She had been endowed with a substantial superstructure and once explained to a visitor who had favorably commented on Cornelia's beauty and her exquisite figure, "All us Folsoms got big t _ _ _ _."

Ruby was described as being very congenial when she was not drinking but could get mean and vulgar when she was not sober. She was described as having a longtime drinking problem and underwent alcohol rehab on several occasions which she described as the "kill-or-cure place," meaning they either kill or cure you while you are there.

Once she and her current boyfriend showed up at the wrong house for a Christmas party but when informed that they were having a party, Big Ruby invited themselves into the party and made a shambles of it.

Ruby had a face lift when she got older and after a favorable recovery stated, "I like it so much I'm thinking about having my body tightened up, too."

Ruby had a bad habit of telling family secrets, so George and Cornelia made her swear off from talking to the press during the 1972 presidential campaign. An enterprising and attractive young female reporter for the *Chicago Tribune* kept after Ruby for an interview, and she finally was invited to go with her to the regular Wednesday night meeting with her friends at the Diplomat Hotel. She told the young reporter, "Let's go out to the Diplomat. Maybe I can get you laid too."

She later told the same reporter, "I just love the PTL club and every morning I promise the Lord I'm going to stop drinking, but by mid-day I start backsliding."

She once related that she had gotten pregnant with Cornelia when she went to see a movie and heard Nelson Eddy sing "Indian Love Call" and got so excited that she went home and got impregnated by her husband who she woke up from a sound sleep. As to her drinking she stated, "The Folsom's drank. I have a hollow leg and I drink, and I'm a Folsom. I'm not proud of it, and I don't fight it."

When she was asked how she wanted to be buried she said, "Put a glass with some Coffee County branch water and bourbon in it. Dress me up, put a bottle of Jack Daniels on my left hip, put my left hand on the bottle, and I'll be ready for Heaven."

When she died in 2000 at the age of eighty-seven she was buried in Enterprise, Coffee County, Alabama at the Evergreen Cemetery in her home town of Elba. With her death Alabama lost one of its most colorful and outspoken personalities. Many a politician did a sigh of relief that her secrets about them went with her to the grave.

FIGHTIN' SHORTY PRICE & GEORGE WALLACE

One of the most unusual characters to come out of the State of Alabama would be William Ralph "Shorty" Price from Louisville, Barbour County, better known as "Fightin Shorty Price." Price had been a roommate of George Corley Wallace for one semester at the University of Alabama before World War II and initially would help Wallace in campus and Barbour County politics, but they had a falling out in George's first campaign for governor in 1958 when Wallace ran against Phenix City Attorney John Patterson as the "fighting little judge."

Shorty Price ran against Wallace for governor in 1958 following him around the state and harassing George in many ways. One of Shorty's tactics was to yell at Wallace, "Stand up George, and let 'em see I'm littler than you (Shorty was 'four foot twelve') and tell 'em I can fight better 'n you." Starting in 1950, after he dropped out of Alabama Law School, Shorty ran for governor, lieutenant governor, Congress, the State House of Representatives, delegate and alternate delegate to the Democratic National Convention and presidential election. He never won an election but was proud of the fact that he finished sixth in a seven candidate race for governor in 1970.

A newspaper editor for a local paper wrote a feature story on Shorty's sixth place finish with headlines "BEATS BROWN IN GOV. RACE" Over the years his relationship with George Wallace ran both hot and cold. He would harass Wallace in the 1958, 1966 and 1970 governor's race and support him in 1964 for president by blanketing the Auburn campus with cards supporting George that read, "I'm for George Wallace all the way – Let's put a white man in the White House." Shorty got arrested for urinating on the sidewalk in Montgomery and was fined ten dollars by the judge. Shorty's complaint to the police was, "You treat horses and dogs better than you treat people."

Another incident in Montgomery was when he was stopped pushing his car down a public street on inauguration day for a new governor and when questioned by the police he told the officers, "I was too drunk to drive." Shorty was arrested for public drunkenness thirty times in thirty-four years by the Birmingham police. When he was arrested in 1980, he offered the defense, "Being drunk at a University of Alabama football game was a natural state." Shorty's antics at Crimson Tide football games sometimes landed him in jail.

In 1979 after he pleaded guilty to public intoxication and disorderly conduct charges following the Alabama-Tennessee game at Legion Field, the sentencing judge fined him $125 dollars and remarked, "See you next fall."

One of his campaign outfits was wearing a red and white suit adorned with the words "Roll Tide." Another of his campaign slogans was, "Smoke Tampa Nugget cigars; drink Budweiser beer and vote for Shorty Price."

Shorty called George Wallace "Little Jesus" in the 1970 race and kicked off his campaign by having his five-year-old daughter lead a Barbour County crowd in a cheer, "Shorty, Shorty, he's our man. George Wallace belongs in a garbage can."

In 1966 Delores Price, Shorty's wife, was the first woman to run for governor of Alabama. It was also the race that George Wallace couldn't succeed himself as governor, so he was planning to run his wife Lurleen as a stand-in for him. The fact that Delores was only twenty-three-years old and was seven years too young to run for the office under the thirty-year-old requirement didn't deter her and Shorty.

Wallace's opponents decided to give Shorty and Delores five hundred dollars to buy some new clothes and harass George. Campaign literature was prepared bearing a photograph of Shorty and Delores with their heads together under campaign slogans, "Two hearts that beat as one," and "The Prices are Right." For a book *I Ain't Nothing But a Loser: The Hard Life of Shorty Price, Alabama's "Head Cheerleader"* that Shorty paid to have published in 1973, he asked a Republican Congressman from Opelika to send him ten dollars and he would send him a copy of the book. When the Congressman only sent Shorty five dollars, the author said, "Send him half a book."

Wallace had been beaten by Patterson because his opponent was running as a staunch segregationist. It was this defeat that allegedly caused Wallace to make the remark, "John Patterson out-n _ _ _ _ _ _ _ me, but I won't be out-n _ _ _ _ _ _ _ again." The defeat launched Wallace as a third party candidate for president in 1964, 1968 and 1972.

In 1970 Shorty ran for governor on a platform to reduce the term of governor from four years to two with the statement, "If you can't steal enough to last you the rest of your life, you ain't got enough sense to have the office in the first place."

Shorty Price was never a powerful and successful politician, but he was a character who was an important part of southern political and historical folklore in the rich history of colorful candidates in the South. Shorty died in an automobile accident at the age of fifty-nine on November 1, 1980. What Shorty did in a humorous way some modern-day politicians accomplish the same results when they try to be serious!

PHENIX CITY – ORIGINAL SIN CITY

Before the popular television show "Sin City" came into existence depicting Las Vegas, Nevada's lifestyle, the original sin city during the era of 1910-1960 was what is now a small family-oriented community in Lee and Russell counties in the State of Alabama – Phenix City.

This small township had a population of 32,822 residents in the 2010 census and in 2007 was selected by *Business Week Magazine* as the nation's #1 Best Affordable Suburb to raise a family. Such was not the case in the pre-war years in the little town across the Chattahoochee River connecting it to Columbus, Georgia, home of the large Army base, Fort Benning.

For years Phenix City had thrived with an underworld culture, corrupt law enforcement, and crooked governments. Due to the positive economic impact and Robin Hood philanthropy of the operators of the illegal establishments, the local citizenry had been unable to oust the criminal element that promoted gambling, prostitution, illegal whiskey operations, drugs, white slavery, and murder. Soldiers from Fort Benning provided an ample supply of young men eager to spend their government checks on the whiskey, women, and crooked games of chance in Phenix City.

During its first half of its existence, it was widely known as the most corrupt city in the nation. From 1945 to 1954 the town was the home of 1,000 prostitutes. The reputation of the town was so corrupt that General George Patten while stationed at Fort Benning once threatened to roll his tanks across the river and destroy Phenix City in 1940. However, the sinful reputation of the community had existed for nearly 100 years. In 1917 during World War I, it had the nation's highest rate of venereal diseases. The construction and opening of Fort Benning in 1918 provided a new market of young soldiers to engage in the sinful activities.

A courageous lawyer form Phenix City, Albert Patterson, Sr., realized that there was no chance of stopping the corruption at the local level and decided that the State of Alabama would have to take action. He chose to run for the position of Attorney General of the entire state on a platform of cleaning up Phenix City. He won the democratic nomination in June of 1954 which virtually assured him of being elected attorney general in the fall general election.

The crime syndicate running Phenix City knew that, with Patterson having the power of the State of Alabama behind him, it could bring the end of their power in the community. On June 18, 1954, after his primary victory, he was gunned down in the alley where he parked his car near his law office.

A county deputy chief, Albert Fuller, was later convicted of the murder and sentenced to life in prison but only served ten years. The assistant district attorney, Silas Garrett, was indicted but fled to the State of Texas and checked into a mental institution. A third defendant, county attorney, Archer Ferrell Garrett, was acquitted in a jury trial.

Rather than solving their problems with the murder of Albert Patterson, the crime machine in Phenix City aroused the anger of President Dwight Eisenhower, FBI Director J. Edgar Hoover, and law enforcement across the nation. As a result, the Governor of Alabama, Gordon Persons, declared "limited martial rule" and the National Guard took over law enforcement from local officials. They raided businesses, seized equipment, and wiped out the crime syndicate.

In the following crack down on crime, 749 indictments against 150 individuals were returned by the local reorganized grand jury, and all but two of the defendants pled guilty or were found guilty by a trial jury.

John Patterson, the thirty-two year old son of Albert, replaced his father as State Attorney General and later became Governor in 1958 defeating George C. Wallace. Patterson's tough stance against integration was responsible for his victory over the more progressive Wallace who vowed he would never lose another race for that reason, and Wallace immediately turned into a staunch segregationist.

The story of Phenix City has been memorialized in both literature and film. The *Columbia Ledger Enquirer* won a Pulitzer Prize for its longtime reporting of the corruption in Phenix City both before and after the Patterson killing.

The Tragedy and Triumph of Phenix City, Alabama by Margaret Anne Barnes and *When Good Men Do Nothing: The Assassination of Albert Patterson* by Allan Grady provide written documentation of the events in that era.

Turner Classic Movies (TCM) will periodically show the 1955 black and white film *The Phenix City Story* during its movie series. It was filmed on location in Phenix City, and many local residents were selected to play in the film, including the female operator of one of the town's favorite nights clubs and brothel.

Although being chosen an "All American City" shortly after the corruption clean-up by the National Civic League, Phenix City still has had to bear the stigma of being called the "Wickedest City in America" for decades into the future.

JOHN M. PATTERSON – ALABAMA GOVERNOR (1921)

John M. Patterson was the son of Albert Patterson who was assassinated outside of his law office in Phenix City, Alabama shortly after he had won the Democratic nomination for Alabama Attorney General on a campaign agenda of elimination of corruption that had existed in the city for over 100 years.

Born on September 27, 1921, John served in WWII. Enlisting in 1940 in the U.S. Army as a private, he rose through the ranks to attain the rank of Major with a Bronze Star in 1945.

He graduated from law school at the University of Alabama in 1949 and joined his father's law practice in Phenix City. Recalled to the military during the Korean conflict in December, 1953, he later rejoined his father's practice.

After his father was killed on June 18, 1954, John was elected State Attorney General in 1955. John Patterson campaigned for governor on three main issues in 1958.

1) The cleanup of Phenix City
2) Investigations of corruption in the second administration of governor James E. Folsom, Jr. and
3) Legal attempts to prevent desegregation

Although he was a populist and attempted reform in the areas of property tax assessment and education, it is in his dedicated fight against integration that he is best remembered. In that capacity, he clashed with the John F. Kennedy administration over the handling of the Freedom Riders who came to Alabama to assist in desegregation efforts. In 1958 he vigorously opposed mixing of the races, and he was able to portray George C. Wallace as a moderate on the subject.

After his defeat, Wallace is alleged to have stated, "This will be the last time I will be out n_ _ _ _ _ _ _ in a political campaign." Wallace assumed the hard line against integration which would ultimately lead to national prominence on that single issue. Patterson won the run off with Wallace and received 55% of the vote with support of the Klu Klux Klan, organized labor, and working class white votes.

When Patterson entered the Governor's office, he fought hard for improving education and the revision of the property tax assessment program with limited success.

After he left office he was part of the trio of himself, Ryan de Graffenried, and U. S. Senator John Sparkman that fought the Alabama Senates' passage of the successor amendment which would have allowed a Governor to serve two consecutive terms of office. This political fight affected Alabama politics for many years and led to the defeat of many Patterson supporters in the Alabama Legislature.

Patterson ran for the Alabama Supreme Court in 1970 but lost to future U.S. Senator Howell Heflin of Tuscumbia, Alabama.

Governor George Wallace in 1984 appointed John to the intermediate Court of Criminal Appeals where he was elected for two terms and retired in 1997.

When ouster proceedings were filed against controversial Alabama Supreme Court Justice Roy Moore, Patterson was sworn in as Special Chief Justice where he presided over the court that upheld the decision of the Alabama Court of Judiciary to remove Moore from judicial office.

After completing this public service he retired to his place of birth in Goldville on the family farm. In 2008 the University of Alabama Press published Gene Howard's, *Patterson for Alabama: The Life and Career of John Patterson.*

JAMES EDWIN HORTON, JR.
BRAVEST JUDGE IN LEGAL HISTORY

Most of the legal decisions that establish new precedents or expansion of civil liberties are usually handed down by appellate judges and not by trial judges. The reasons for this are numerous:

1. Appellate judges are usually removed from the local notoriety of highly sensational cases. They normally hear cases at some distance from the actual trial. The hearings at which attorneys argue the merits of a conviction are usually poorly attended in contrast to the actual trial in the community where the alleged crime took place;

2. The presence of cameras in the courtroom and the competing television stations vying for news coverage often put intense pressure upon the parties participating in a trial.

In 1933 the United States Supreme Court had reversed the death penalty convictions of the nine black teenage males charged with gang rape of two white women on a freight train near Paint Rock, Alabama, outside the county seat of Scottsboro. The defendants, forever to be known as the "Scottsboro Boys," had won a new trial on the grounds that their constitutional rights to a competent defense has been denied in their original trials two years earlier.

The second trial would be held in Decatur, Alabama, where fifty-five year old Circuit Judge James Edwin Horton, Jr., presided. Judge Horton had served as circuit judge since 1922 and had overwhelmingly been re-elected for a second term of office.

The new trials to be held in Decatur were only fifteen miles from Judge Horton's home in Athens. Known as a fair judge by the attorneys who practiced before him, Judge Horton was determined that the defendants would get a fair trial in spite of the tense public sentiment against them.

Judge Horton initially denied the defense motion to dismiss the charges on the grounds of the systematic exclusion of Negroes from county grand jury rolls. A similar motion attacking the method of selection in trial jurors that excluded blacks was also made and denied.

In spite of many discrepancies in the testimony of one of the victims, Victoria Price, the lack of specific medical evidence and the surprise favorable testimony for the defense of the other alleged rape victim, Ruby Bates, the jury quickly found the first defendant to be tried, Haywood Patterson, guilty of murder. He was sentenced to die in the electric chair.

Judge Horton took the unusual and highly controversial step of granting Patterson a new trial on the grounds of the jury's verdict being contrary to the sufficiency of the evidence.

When the motion was called in court, Judge Horton did not call for any argument by counsel for either side, and he digressed into reading a typewritten transcript for sixty-five minutes.

Horton would later admit that he was told by an emissary from Montgomery, Alabama, that if he should overturn the verdict of the jury and grant a new trial that he would have little or no chance of being re-elected. Yet Judge Horton demonstrated tremendous courage in spite of intense public pressure when he granted Patterson a new trial.

Following his decision, Judge Horton hoped that the prosecution would drop the case against Patterson and the other defendants. However the political ambitions of District Attorney General Thomas Knight and the atmosphere against the Scottsboro Boys prevented the request from happening.

Judge Horton granted a continuance of the next trial against Charles Weems in an effort to let things cool down, but the only result was to allow D.A. Knight to effectively have Judge Horton removed from hearing any more of the cases by the Alabama Supreme Court.

In 1934 Horton was defeated when he ran for re-election by a vote of 9,416 for his opponent, while Horton received 6,856 votes.

Subsequent to his defeat he became a successful farmer and cattleman and died in March 1973, at age ninety-five.

Throughout the history of the judiciary in both Alabama and America, never has any jurist matched the courage of Judge James Edwin Horton, Jr., in the Scottsboro Boys case of Haywood Patterson.

Judge Horton's family motto was *Justitia Fiat Caelum* ("May justice be done, though the Heavens fall.") He certainly followed its dictates in his judiciary duties in 1933.

Judge James Edwin Horton, Jr.

WORST JUDGE WHO PRESIDED OVER THE SCOTTSBORO BOYS TRIALS WILLIAM WASHINGTON CALLAHAN

Much has been written about the judicial courage displayed by Judge James Horton in the recorded trial of the Scottsboro Boys in Decatur, Alabama, after the first convictions before Judge E. A. Hawkins in Scottsboro was overturned by the United States Supreme Court on November 7, 1931, on grounds of ineffective assistance of counsel appointed to represent the defendants.

Following a second conviction after Judge Horton had granted the defendants a new trial because of insufficient evidence, the cases were transferred to the division of Judge William Callahan.

The Alabama Supreme Court removed Horton at the request of politically ambitious District Attorney Thomas Knight. Knight would ultimately be elected lieutenant governor of Alabama while Judge Horton would be defeated for re-election after setting aside the guilty verdict in the Hayward Patterson case.

William Callahan was born in 1863 on a farm in Lawrence County, Alabama and never received any formal training to become an attorney. He acquired his knowledge of the law working in the office of a Decatur, Alabama law firm. He had served as the city solicitor of Decatur and had been a member of the Alabama legislature prior to being elected circuit judge in 1928. He was seventy years old when he was assigned to the Scottsboro Boys cases and would preside over them from November 1933 to July 1937.

Whereas Horton had tried to ensure that the defendants received a fair trial in the highly volatile and violet atmosphere surrounding the alleged charges of the nine young black men of raping two white women while hoboing on a freight train from Chattanooga to Memphis, Judge Callahan acted just the opposite.

Callahan was known as a gruff, no nonsense and racist judge.

Horton, having little respect for Callahan, had unsuccessfully asked the Chief Justice of the Alabama Supreme Court to appoint a judge from outside the judicial district who might be more prone to give the defendants fair trials.

Although Judge Callahan fit the prototype of a southern judge with his broad shoulders, silver hair and glasses, he also projected the imagine of a white supremacist that would have little tolerance for Samuel Lebowitz, the Jewish New York City chief trial counsel for the defendants.

Whereas Horton had allowed the parties to try their case in a fair and impartial manner, Callahan assumed the role of being a second prosecutor for the state. He sustained virtually all of the prosecutor's objections while overruling nearly all of those by the defense. Ignoring prior rulings by Judge Horton, he castigated and criticized Attorney Lebowitz in his zeal to help the prosecution obtain a conviction.

On the few occasions that the prosecution did not object to some testimony, Callahan would make a spontaneous ruling from the bench in the absence of the prosecution asking him to rule favorably for its side of the case. He limited cross-examination by the defense as to the bad reputation of alleged victim, Victoria Price.

Perhaps the biggest contrast between his and Judge Horton's rulings on the admissible evidence arose when Callahan refused to allow the defense to introduce evidence that the semen found in Victoria Price may have come from prior sexual relations two days before the date of the alleged assault.

Eventually the most important adverse ruling that Callahan made was overruling the defense motions to dismiss the charges because blacks had been excluded from the jury rolls in Jackson County, Alabama. This ruling would lead to a second reversal of the cases by the United States Supreme Court.

Litigation and publicity involving the Scottsboro Boys would continue into 1976 when the last of the defendants, Clarence Norris, was pardoned by the State of Alabama in 1976. In 1989 He was also the last defendant to die.

Judge Horton paid a political price of being defeated for re-election for attempting to give the defendants a fair trial. Judge Callahan enjoyed public acclaim for his bigotry and prejudicial judicial conduct in assisting the State of Alabama to obtain convictions.

THOMAS E. KNIGHT SCOTTSBORO PROSECUTOR

In 1935 the United States Supreme Court issued the landmark decision of Berger v. New York (1935.) "It is as much the duty of the United States Attorney (prosecutor) to refrain from improper methods calculated to produce a wrongful conviction as it is to use every legitimate means to bring about a just one." The decision plus the actions of the American Bar Association and state courts in adopting rules of ethical conduct for judges, prosecutors, and defense counsel corrected many unscrupulous tactics employed by overzealous members of the three groups to insure a fair trial for all parties.

Unfortunately those rules were not in force when the Scottsboro Boys came to trial in Scottsboro, Alabama in March 1931. The combination of improper action by Judge Hawkins in the first trial, and Judge Callahan in the third trial, after Judge Horton had tried unsuccessfully to give the defendants a fair trial, was also enhanced by the continued bigotry and political ambition of Attorney General Thomas E. Knight who handled the prosecution.

Thomas E. Knight, Jr. was born in 1898 in Greensboro, Alabama, the son of Thomas E. Knight, Sr., who would later serve as a justice on the Alabama Supreme Court and who wrote the majority opinion in 1932 upholding the verdicts and death sentences in the initial Scottsboro trials. He was also the 19th Attorney General of Alabama from 1931 to 1935 and in that capacity took over the prosecution from the local District Attorney. He would also unsuccessfully defend his father's opinion in oral arguments before the United States Supreme Court. It is highly probable that today a son could not be on a case where the father was also involved in the appeal. He would argue all three appeals in that high court stemming from the trials in 1932 and 1935.

During the two trials, Knight was aggressive and brutally attacked the defense witnesses. His clashes with chief defense council, Samuel Leibowitz of New York, were frequent and heated. He was particularly offended by Leibowitz's tactics of attacking the Alabama jury system for not having black members as an "attack on the sovereignty" of the State of Alabama. His courtroom antics of getting in the faces of defense witnesses and raising his voice to a shout while sticking a finger within a few inches of the person's face, was highly improper but popular with the members in the audience who were heavily pro-prosecution.

His most serious ethical violation was convincing the Alabama Supreme Court in private to remove Judge Horton from any future cases after the justice had granted Haywood Patterson a new trial in the second case. Knight rode his victories to new political heights. He served as the 13th Lieutenant Governor of Alabama from 1935 to 1937. His main political goal was to be elected Governor of the State, but he died suddenly in Montgomery, Alabama on May 17, 1937, due to complication from kidney and liver conditions.

Knight, whether because of the reversal of the convictions, or for political reasons, made a decision to try and resolve the cases after the final Supreme Court reversals in 1936. He secretly met with Samuel Leibowitz in New York to discuss a possible compromise. He allegedly told Leibowitz that he was "sick of the cases" and that they were causing Alabama considerable political and economic harm. Leibowitz later stated that Knight had finally come to the conclusion that the women who were the alleged victims were lying and that no rape had taken place.

Knight was willing to dismiss the rape charges against four of the defendants and to allow the others to plead guilty to a reduced charge of assault with credit for jail time served at either the local jails or Kilby Prison. Unfortunately the compromise was never put into effect because of Knight dying on May 17, 1937. His successor, A. A. Carmichael feared "looking soft" on crime and never settled or tried the cases again.

As a result, the cases lingered on in the Alabama Justice system. It was thought that Governor Bibb Graves would end the tragedy of the Scottsboro Boys by granting the five remaining defendants parole before he left office, and after Graves had conducted his traditional pre-pardon interviews with each in his office. However, the defendants made such horrible witnesses, and because none of them admitted any knowledge or guilt concerning a rape aboard the Chattanooga to Memphis freight train, Graves left office without issuing the pardons.

Either through paroles or escapes, all of the Scottsboro defendants left the State of Alabama. In 1976, the last surviving Scottsboro Boy, Clarence Norris, received a full pardon signed by former avid segregationist, Governor George C. Wallace. Norris published a book entitled *The Last of the Scottsboro Boys*. He died on January 23, 1989, as the last survivor of the nine young black men who had to go through their horrible experiences.

In spite of the injustice done to these illiterate young victims, changes did take place that corrected some of the mistakes of the Scottsboro and Decatur trials. Blacks now sit on juries in Alabama, and the cause of civil rights made gradual but steady progress that would result in the Civil Rights Acts of 1964 and 1968. Unfortunately it would take the ordeals of the Scottsboro Boys and the death of Martin Luther King to create such progress.

CHATTANOOGANS AT SCOTTSBORO BOYS' TRIALS

Much has been written about the historic Scottsboro Boys Trial which started the revolution of civil rights in America for many African Americans in 1931.

It is well documented that on March 25, 1931 nine Negroes were charged with the rape of two white women, Victoria Price, and Ruby Bates, while all were hoboing on a freight train from Chattanooga to Memphis. The alleged crime occurred in Jackson County, Alabama, where Scottsboro is the county seat and site of the first famous trial.

From that date until the last three of the nine defendants were pardoned by the Alabama Parole Board on November 21, 2013, and their convictions were stricken from court records, the cases were an unpleasant reminder of the mistreatment and inability of blacks to receive justice in Alabama. The last defendant had died in 1989 in Detroit, Michigan.

Two books stand out amongst the publications about the Scottsboro Boys trials. Dan Carter's *Scottsboro,* Louisiana State Press (1986) and James Goodman's *Stories of Scottsboro* Vintage Books (1994) are the most authoritatively correct.

The Chattanooga legal community was involved in the case early on by Attorney Stephen Roddy and then George W. Chamblee. A third attorney, Raulston Schoolfield, has been alleged to have been asked to join the defense team in the second trial when Samuel Leibowitz was retained by the International Legal Defense (ILD), but he disagreed with the trial strategy advocated by the New York attorney of attacking the community and the two white girls, and he did not become involved.

Stephen Roddy was born in Centralia, Missouri on March 13, 1890 and came to Chattanooga in 1910 to attend the Chattanooga College of Law. He remained in Chattanooga after graduation and was employed by the law firm headed by Justice Alexander W. Chambliss of the Tennessee Supreme Court, prior to serving in World War I. Roddy was active and prominent in Democratic politics at both the local and state levels.

In 1926 he was a candidate for attorney general of Hamilton County. He ran against the incumbent J.J. Lively and George W. Chamblee in a three man race of the Democratic nomination. He ran second to Lively by less than one hundred votes.

When the Scottsboro case arose in March 1931, Roddy was approached by black ministers in Chattanooga in the Interdenominational Ministers Alliance to go to Scottsboro and observe the trial. He was paid $50.00 for his services. When Judge A. E. Hawkins called the cases in Alabama, no local attorney spoke up for the defendants, and Roddy stepped forward. He and a local sixty-nine-year-old attorney, Milo Moody, of limited legal ability, suddenly became the defense team under unusual circumstances. Roddy attempted to avoid the appointment by claiming he did not want to try the case alone, but the judge kept him on the case when Moody offered to assist him.

Roddy and Moody put on a limited defense which was later declared by the United State Supreme Court to be "ineffective assistance of counsel" and a "denial of due process" in November 1932, when the Supreme Court reversed the death sentences imposed by the jury on seven of the defendants.

The two attorneys, under trying conditions, had only been able to give perfunctory representation to the defendants. One case had been declared a mistrial, and the juvenile, Eugene Williams, had his conviction reversed because he was under age in 1931.

As a result of the verdicts, two competing organizations: the International Labor Defense (ILD), a communist propaganda group, and the National Association for the Advancement of Colored people (NAACP), attempted to take over the cases on behalf of the defendants by volunteering to represent them. Roddy had declined to stay on the case when he was informed that the fees would be raised by holding mass meetings among Negroes.

Clarence Darrow, famous in Tennessee for his participation in the John Scopes evolution trial in Dayton, Tennessee in 1925, had been approached about entering the case to file an appeal to the Alabama Supreme Court. The internal bickering between the ILD and NAACP for control of the case ultimately led to a decision by Darrow to decline to enter an appearance in the case, and he had no further involvement in any of the future legal proceedings. Prior to leaving the case and turning down a $5,000.00 fee to argue the appeal in the Alabama Supreme Court, Darrow expressed concerns that the friction between the two groups was jeopardizing any chance for a reversal of the verdicts on appeal.

The ILD promised the Chattanooga Negro Ministers Alliance that it would take over the entire financial burden of the case. Although some of the ministers wanted to keep the first attorney on the case, Roddy was eventually replaced by attorney George W. Chamblee, Sr., former district attorney in Hamilton County during 1918-1926.

Chamblee was employed by the ILD to take over the defense of the case along with Samuel Leibowitz, and he was heavily involved in several of the trials that took place in Alabama. Although Chamblee was a grandson of a decorated Confederate veteran and a member of a prominent Tennessee family, he was an individual who had no problem in representing unpopular defendants and causes, including communists and radicals. His selection by the ILD led to further accusations against the ILD by the NAACP as "the legal arm of the Communist Party.

Efforts to gain control of the defense by both organizations would continue through the trials and appeals over the years.

Chamblee had been born in 1872 in Canton, Georgia, and after graduating from Mercer Law School, he came to Chattanooga and practiced with his three brothers until his death. He served the community as both city attorney of Chattanooga for six years and as district attorney general from 1918 to 1929. He represented many moonshiners during the Prohibition Era and claimed that he had tried over 800 murder cases with none of his clients ever being electrocuted or hung.

Although Chamblee's role in the famous trials in Scottsboro is much more extensive than Roddy's, the fact that the unfortunate train trip originated in Chattanooga and the defendants' presence in the legal process established a significant connection between our community and the historic events in Alabama.

Chamblee and a lawyer from New York, Joseph Brodsky, argued the first appeal in the Alabama Supreme Court on January 21, 1932. Chamblee devoted his allotted time to the issue of the defendant's defense counsel's inadequate performance during the trial. On March 24, 1932, the Alabama Supreme Court denied the appeal.

Chamblee was soon joined by attorney Samuel Leibowitz of New York who would assume the responsibility of much of the future trial work on behalf of the defendants after the first United States Supreme Court reversal of the Hayward Patterson death sentence. Unfortunately, Leibowitz's "Yankee style" of trying criminal cases did not appeal to a jury that was comprised of eight Alabama farmers and four other males.

Leibowitz would continue to gain a reputation as an excellent criminal defense lawyer and would become a trial judge in New York. In spite of his career as a vigorous defender of defendants, he developed a controversial reputation of being a "hanging judge" in sentencing defendants. He strongly believed in capital punishment.

Accusations were later made against Chamblee that he had paid witnesses to sign false post-trial affidavits concerning prosecution witnesses, Ruby Bates and Victoria Price. His legal predecessor, Stephen Roddy, still angry that he had been pushed out of the case in favor of Chamblee, filed a complaint with the Chattanooga Bar Association asking that Chamblee be disbarred for "conspiracy and interference with pending court proceedings." However, the investigation absolved Chamblee of any wrongdoing.

George W. Chamblee practiced law in Chattanooga until 1958 when he died at the age of 85 after coming to the city in 1893. During the Prohibition Era he had become famous for his defense of hundreds of moonshiners in federal court.

Active in many Masonic, patriotic, and religious organizations, he adopted the role of writing with warmth and affection about lawyers who had passed.

Chamblee was not mentioned in the Public Broadcasting System documentary on video titled "Scottsboro, An American Tragedy", in 2001. However, he was a participant in the 2006 movie, *Heavens Fall* featuring Academy Award Winner Timothy Hutton as Samuel Leibowitz. Bill Smitrovich portrayed George Chamblee as he had actively participated in the trial featured in the film.

Another Chattanoogan who participated in one of the famous rape cases was Dr. Edward Reisman, a gynecologist. He testified for the defense in the second trial that the physical facts and the medical examination did not support the allegations of one of the women that she had been sexually assaulted by six of the black defendants. In spite of Dr. Reisman's testimony and the inconclusive testimony of both of the initial examining physicians, Dr. R. R. Bridges and Dr. Marvin Lynch, the defendants were convicted.

Another alleged part of the story is that Judge Horton and Dr. Lynch secretly met *ex parte* (outside the presence of both sides' attorneys) in the men's restroom, and discussed that the physician could not conclusively confirm that Bates/Price had been raped by the defendants. However, he expressed great concern to Judge Horton that his medical practice in Scottsboro would be destroyed if he testified favorably on behalf of the defendants.

After Dr. Bridges testified for the prosecution, the State of Alabama, as Dr. Lynch was to take stand, "he asked Judge Horton to excuse him, arguing that his testimony would only be a repetition of Bridges."

Although the radically prejudiced atmosphere would (and did) preclude any not-guilty verdicts on behalf of the defendants, it is still puzzling that experienced and capable trial lawyers like Leibowitz and Chamblee could be lulled into such a prosecution tactic.

Evidently Dr. Lynch's disclosure to Judge Horton played a big part in the jurists' surprise decision to grant a new trial. Judge James E.

Horton, in an act of unparalleled judicial courage, made a decision granting the defendants a new trial which would ultimately lead to his defeat at the next election.

All three Chattanoogans played an important part in the historic series of tragic trials.

THE DRANO MURDER CASE – A LAWYER'S PRICE
ROBERT B. FRENCH, JR.

One of the most notorious criminal cases in the State of Alabama occurring in September 1982 was the rape and capital murder cases involving defendants, Alvin Howard Neelley, Jr. and his teenage bride wife, Judith Ann Neelley, and a thirteen year old victim, Lisa Millican, who had run away from an orphanage outing at the Riverbend Mall in Rome, Georgia.

Lisa had been enticed into sexual captivity by Judith Ann Neelley as part of a bizarre scheme whereby she attempted to lure young girls and young women into the car with her for the ultimate purpose of making them available to her husband for involuntary acts.

This crime spree also included a separate Janice Chapman murder on October 4, 1982 in Rome, Georgia of another young female and the non-fatal shooting of her male companion John Hancock in a wooded area in Catoosa County in northwest Georgia.

The victim in the Alabama case had been taken to the Little River Canyon rim above Fort Payne on September 28, 1982 and was handcuffed to a tree. Lisa was injected six times with liquid cleaner (Drano) and then shot in the back. After the fatal shot, her body was thrown into the canyon.

The facts of these crimes and others committed by Alvin Neelley and his pregnant teenage wife, Judith Ann, are described in a lengthy opinion of the Court of Criminal Appeals of Alabama in the case of Judith Ann Neelley v. State, 494 So.2d 669 (1985).

After a six-week sensational trial, Judith Ann was found guilty of capital murder in Fort Payne by a jury and sentenced to life without parole. The verdict was changed by the trial judge, Randall Cole to death by electrocution.

After exhausting her appeals, the female murderer's sentence was commuted back to life without parole by Alabama Governor Republican Fob James on the last day of his administration. This would lead to the Alabama Legislature passing a law that prohibits parole for any inmate whose death sentence was commuted to life. However, a federal judge ruled that the law could not be applied retroactively to Judith Ann Neelley.

Alvin Neelley had been charged as an accomplice to his wife's deadly acts and allowed to plead guilty. He was sentenced to life imprisonment in Georgia and would die in prison at Milledgeville, Georgia in 2005. He was not tried on the Alabama case of Lisa Millican. His wife would also plead to a life sentence in the Georgia murder.

In May 2018 Judith Ann Neelley waived her first appearance before the Alabama Board of Pardons and Paroles after her commutation from the death penalty. The Board denied the automatic petition in about a minute after an earlier hearing on an impassioned public plea from Alabama Governor Kay Ivey who stated, "Neelley, age 53, should never be paroled."

Attorney Robert B. French, Jr. of Fort Payne was also a victim in the case. A successful trial lawyer, he had acquired all of the material benefits of favorable results in both criminal and civil results over the years. Airplanes, luxurious automobiles, real estate and a reputation of being an outstanding lawyer were all part of Bob French's standing in the community. He had also been teaching the Baraca Bible Class at the First Baptist Church in Fort Payne for 17 years when he got a call from Circuit Judge Randall Cole appointing him to represent Mrs. Neelley.

French was one of the few Republicans in Democrat dominated Alabama in 1982. He had run unsuccessfully for public office three times on the GOP ticket. He was narrowly defeated for Congress in 1964, ran for Lt. Governor in 1970, and he also ran for the Alabama Supreme Court in 1988.

He attempted to get out of the appointment of Judge Cole, as the judge had previously reported him to the Ethics Committee of the

Alabama Bar Association. French was acquitted of the accusation, but the judge stated, "If you can't agree to take the case, I may have to order you to take it."

Thus, began the court appointment that would adversely affect the veteran lawyer's life forever. Alabama at the time of the Drano murder did not have a government financed Public Defenders Office. The State relied upon members of the legal profession to represent, by court appointment, individuals that could not afford to hire an attorney to defend them. The State provided the maximum sum of $500.00 to approved lawyers for their efforts. (Bob French did not get his $500).

In a book titled *Beaten, Battered and Damned. The Drano Murder Trial* published in 1989, French describes the ordeal that he went through in his belief that "Anyone charged in a criminal case in America is entitled to be represented by an attorney."

The stress of fighting to save his client's life caused him to have a serious eye problem; his home was rocked by night riders; his law office was picketed by protesters; and he received lots of hate mail. His three children were harassed at school, and he was asked by some church members to quit teaching his Sunday School class.

French bordered on the brink of financial disaster, incurred investigation and expert witness costs in excess of half a million dollars, went in debt, and finally had to file a Chapter 11 reorganization plan in Bankruptcy Court. His home was foreclosed upon and his law practice diminished substantially. The most serious and vicious attacks on his reputation were the rumors that he was in love with Neelley, had sex with her and was the father of her unborn child, although she was already pregnant when French was appointed to represent her.

Yet within 36 months he had paid off his debts and in 1990 was honored as the number one Criminal Defense Lawyer in Alabama. Today at the age of 87 he is still practicing law in his hometown of Fort Payne. The Dedication in the book about the Drano Murder is to "Criminal Defense Lawyers who represent shockingly evil clients."

It is a story worth reading!

GEORGIA ARTICLES

"DOC" ANDERSON – ROSSVILLE'S PSYCHIC

Psychic, seer, ESP practitioner, clairvoyant astrologer, fake, quack, etc. are all terms used to describe the fascinating life of R.C. "Doc" Anderson, a resident of Rossville, Georgia, who died in March, 1980, in the floodwaters of a raging Chattanooga Creek in the 800 block of Hooker Road in South Chattanooga after leaving his office at 302 Gordon Avenue in Rossville.

Doc had attempted to go through the high water in his Lincoln Continental. When his vehicle flooded, he exited the vehicle and was swept away by the swift current and drowned at the age of 72.

His predictions over the years were claimed to be ninety five percent (95%) accurate, and he developed a reputation as a psychic with a clientele that ranged from ordinary folks to movie stars and successful businessmen.

In 1970 a paper-back novel entitled *The Man Who Sees Tomorrow* by Robert E. Smith, published by the Paperback Library, a division of Coronet Communications, was released and described the colorful life of Doc Anderson.

Robert Charles Anderson was born on April 16, 1908, in the small coal mining community of Enterprise, Iowa. A Sioux Indian tribal medicine man described Robert as having the ability at an early age of "talking with the Great Spirit and having the ability to tell things that will come to pass."

During his early life, Anderson engaged in a variety of occupations that included amateur prize fighter, bullfighter, carnival worker and a circus strong man. When his alleged ability to see into the future became known, Anderson was inundated by wives and parents of service men inquiring as to whether their relatives would survive World War II.

He became an adviser to many movie stars who regularly visited him at his office in Rossville. Doris Day, Vincent Price, Denver Pyle, George Raft, Burl Ives, Clint Walker, Charlton Heston and Eddie Albert were actors who often lived their lives based on Doc's predictions.

Eddie Albert first visited Doc when his career was at a low point. When he first consulted Doc, he felt that he had no future in the acting profession. Anderson advised him that his career would have a resurgence, and shortly thereafter Eddie was hired to perform as the male lead in the long running television show "Green Acres" with Eva Gabor as his co-star.

Anderson was not without his critics, and he had legal problems in 1944 in getting his fortune telling license renewed when he maintained an office at 2110 McCallie Avenue in Chattanooga. Originally his license was denied because his residence was in the State of Georgia in Lakeview, and because he had not been a resident of Chattanooga for six months. However the license was eventually renewed on the grounds that the ordinance was designed to keep gypsies and other transients from practicing their fortune telling profession in Chattanooga and not to put regular operators out of business.

Anderson first obtained international prominence when he foretold several events that he predicted in an interview with the *Walker County Messenger,* a weekly newspaper at LaFayette on Christmas Day, 1944. Doc accurately predicted that Franklin D. Roosevelt would not serve out his fourth term of office as president. FDR did pass away in mid-May, 1945.

He also correctly forecast that World War II with Germany would end in May, 1945, and that our strongest ally, Russia, would become one of our worst enemies in what is now called the Cold War. He foretold of the dropping of the Atomic Bomb on Japan in August, 1945, to end the conflict. He predicted that General Dwight D. Eisenhower would become president of the United States in eight years in 1952 rather than the more widely known General Douglas McArthur.

However he was incorrect in predicting that Alabama Governor George Wallace would become president in 1968, although Doc was accurate is saying Wallace would enter the presidential primaries.

Critics question the failure of Doc Anderson to foresee his own pending death in 1980 as evidence that he was not as qualified to predict the future as his supporters claimed.

One unfinished goal that he had intended to pursue prior to his death was to return to Mexico to engage in the dangerous sport of bullfighting. At the age of 72 he wanted to hear the roar of the crowd shouting to his last "ole." The March 23, 1980, drowning foreclosed the world famous psychic's "Last Big Dream."

WHEN DOLLY AND GEORGE CAME TO RINGGOLD

Most historians of the Civil War would probably think that the most famous event in the Ringgold area would be Confederate General Patrick Cleburne's brilliant defense of Ringgold Gap on November 27, 1863, during the South's retreat from the disastrous defeat of Missionary Ridge resulting from the blunders of General Braxton Bragg on November 25, 1863.

Others might be made proud of the accomplishments of a local son in a farm family, O. Wayne Rollins (1912-1991) who in 1964 bought Orkin Exterminating Company from its family owners.

Yet to country music fans, two of the most significant dates would be May 30, 1966, when Dolly Parton married Carl Dean, and in 1969 when George Jones and Tammy Wynette each entered into their third marriage. Other notables that have tied the knot in the northwest Georgia county seat of Catoosa County have been former Louisiana governor and country music performer Jimmy Davis, who wrote and sang his campaign song of "You Are My Sunshine." A more modern-day groom who married in Ringgold on Valentine's Day was Bob Harvey, a member of the rock and roll group, Jefferson Airplane.

The name of a popular and traditional wedding venue is now the Ringgold Wedding Chapel. The current owners are proud that it's often referred to as "the wedding chapel of the South," but they are quick to say that it may now qualify as "the wedding chapel of the world." Couples often come from Europe, Asia, and the Middle East, since they do not want to be married in the glitter and glamour of Las Vegas, Nevada, at a considerably higher cost for speaking their vows.

For couples interested in tying the knot at a reasonable price and avoiding the glitz of Vegas, the Ringgold Wedding Chapel is a favorable alternative. The current owners quickly point out that they can accommodate the potential brides' and grooms' desired level of ceremony with a wide variety of services at various costs.

Getting married in Ringgold can be achieved by a couple in "one day" by going to the Clerk's office early in the morning (check hours of service) and then coming to the chapel to have the nuptials shortly thereafter, and starting the honeymoon all in less than 24 hours. Although once required, it is no longer mandatory to have a blood test in Georgia prior to marriage.

The original wedding chapel began as an Episcopal Methodist Church in 1845. During the Civil War it was destroyed in the winter of 1863 by Union General William T. Sherman in the Battle of Ringgold Gap. In 1925 the federal government paid a pittance of $600 toward rebuilding the Episcopal Church, and it moved to a new and larger location in 1972.

From 1972 until 1986 the old church was used for storage when a lady by the name of Helen Boyd re-instituted the practice of marrying couples in the old building. After another change in ownership, new management took over in 2017. The new owners have updated the facilities as well as increasing the type of services available during the exchange of wedding vows. They are committed to following the tradition of Helen Boyd who said, "I think people deserve a nice wedding, and a good start. We serve those who do not have the money to afford an extremely nice wedding."

So if you and your beloved want to get married, you might consider, as an alternative to Las Vegas, the Ringgold Wedding Chapel at 7683 Nashville Street, Ringgold, Georgia 30736 (706) 935-8199. It is open Monday-Friday from 9:00 a.m. to 4:00 p.m. and on Saturday-Sunday by appointment only.

You might run into a couple of this generation's county music stars who want to follow in Dolly's and George's footsteps down the aisle.

JUDGE MURPHY CLAGETT "RED" TOWNSEND (1899-1961)

The current controversy over the proposed removal of Confederate officer statues, such as Robert E. Lee in Richmond, Virginia, and Nathan Bedford Forrest in Nashville, Tennessee, was preceded many years ago by the controversy over whether Dade County, Georgia, had in 1860 seceded from not only the Union at the beginning of the Civil War, but had also from the State of Georgia. The rumors circulating about Dade County's historical movement has become known as "the Independent State of Dade" controversy. Is it fact or fiction?

The origin of said alleged move was the dissatisfaction of the residents of Dade County with the State of Georgia's indecision as to whether it was, or was not, going to leave the union. Even though the issue still remains as to whether it did secede from the state, there doesn't still exist any doubt that Dade County did rejoin the state on July 4, 1945. The Atlanta radio station WAGA broadcast the proceedings and included a fictitious re-enactment of the Dade County's state senator allegedly re-creating the withdrawal from the State of Georgia.

Thus we come to the role the Honorable Judge John Murphy Clagett "Red" Townsend (as he was popularly known) played in the festivities on the Fourth of July, 1945, that re-emphasized the controversy. Judge Red Townsend has been credited or blamed with creating the scenario that gained tiny Dade County national publicity in 1945.

Although the question of secession or not remains a topic of discussion, there is no dispute about the fact that on July 4, 1945, the community noisily proclaimed its loyalty to the Union. With an estimated crowd of over 4,000 citizens in attendance, a military band played patriotic tunes. A letter was read from President Harry S. Truman congratulating Dade County on its reentry to the Union with the concluding message from the president of, "Welcome Home Pilgrims."

In an effort to orchestrate the "clever publicity event that was the county's attempt to put Dade on the map," Judge Red Townsend speaking on national radio stated, "This is the Fourth of July! That hasn't meant anything to Dade for more than 85 long years. And in all that time, we've never raised a flag except for the one of a lost, however gallant, cause." Any reference to the Lost Cause would automatically cause controversy (and publicity).

John Murphy Clagett Townsend was born at Wildwood on November 30, 1899. Because of his flaming red hair he was always called "Red." He was related to most of the old families in Dade, and because of those connections in some people's minds, he rose to be the county's most famous and influential son. After attending schools in Dade County he graduated from the Chattanooga College of Law in 1923 and would later receive a Master's degree in Law.

He practiced law in Chattanooga and Dade County with E. B. Baker for about 15 years prior to his colleague succumbing to alcohol. Baker was once recognized as Chattanooga's finest trial lawyer. Red was active in the Methodist Church and numerous civic organizations. He engaged in local politics and served as a member of the Georgia House of Representatives from 1931-1936. In his law practice he also served as an Assistant Attorney General during 1937-1943. In 1947 he became a member of the Georgia Court of Appeals and served until 1961.

Upon his death on October 6, 1961, a memorial tribute in 105 Georgia Appeal Report, pages XXIII – LIV described him as a "Great Georgian" who proclaimed the fundamental promise that the "Bill of Rights" is for every man. It further stated, "He was dedicated to the preservation of the constitutional rights of each prisoner before the Bar, whether he be rich or poor, guilty or innocent."

Prior to his death, Townsend testified as a character witness in the disbarment suit against former Hamilton County Criminal Court Judge Raulston Schoolfield in June 1960, which was brought by the Chattanooga and Tennessee Bar Associations. Judge Townsend stated that if Schoolfield applied to the Georgia Bar for admission to practice in the state, he would sponsor him and sign a character certificate for him. To the lawyers who knew "Red" Townsend, he was an original character throughout his lifetime, a knowledgeable lawyer and judge, and the perfect individual to promote his beloved county of Dade with his July 4, 1945, remarks.

When he died, he was credited with applying the rule of John Wesley: "Do all the good you can…To all the people you can, as long as ever you can."

HOWARD FINSTER – PARADISE GARDEN (1916-2001)

The late unorthodox artist and Baptist preacher Howard Finster built a folk art sculpture garden with over 46,000 artifacts in Summerville, Georgia. If you like the unique and strange art forms of Pablo Picasso, you will find Finster's works of art equally fascinating, except that you will discover the religious theme in each of his numerous creations.

Finster was one of fourteen children born to his parents, William Finster, a sawmill lumberjack, and Lula Alice Henegar Finster in Valley Head, Alabama, in DeKalb County. Howard claimed his first religious experience was at the age of three when he had a vision from his deceased sister Abbie Rose. She came to him on a floating stairway and told him that visions and other religious experiences would continue to play a vital role throughout his life. He had another vision after being "born again" at a Baptist revival at the age of 13. At 15 while he was riding on the back of a wagon, God came to him in another vision and called upon him to be a preacher. Thereafter he began preaching at tent revivals in Alabama, Georgia and Tennessee.

At the age of 19, he married Pauline Freeman and they would have five children. In 1940 he became pastor of Rock Bridge Baptist Church near DeSoto State Park and also preached at other small county churches, baptized convertees to the faith, and washed the feet of churchgoers.

Finster began his first garden park museum in Trion, Georgia, in the late 1940s. It featured an exhibit on the inventions of mankind in which he planned to display one of everything that had ever been invented, models of houses and churches, a pigeon flock and a duck pond.

During 1961 the family moved to Summerville, Georgia, near Valley Head. He bought four acres of land upon which he intended to build the Plant Farm Museum or Paradise Garden, "to show all the wondrous things of God's Creation." It would feature many attractions as "the Bible House", "the Mirror House", "the Hubcap Tower", "the Bicycle Tower", "the Machine Gun Nest", and the largest structure in the complex, the five story "Folk Art Chapel."

It was at this point that he began putting Bible verses on his art because he felt, "They struck in people's heads better that way." This creation would become his most famous accomplishment as he filled the space, previously used as a community dump, with art work constructed with items he rescued from the trash. They would feature items such as bicycles, old jewelry, shoes, medical equipment and anything else he could salvage.

All of the themes in his garden environment are evangelical in nature and express Finster's drive to bring his religious message to the public. As the site developed, it quickly became a popular local tourist attraction. There is a difference in reported stories about Finster as to when he quit preaching. One says that he continued preaching and working odd jobs until 1976. Another source states that he had retired from preaching in 1965 and focused all of his time on improving the Plant Farm Museum. Both sources however agree that in 1976 he had another vision to paint. It consisted of a face in a dab of paint on his thumb that commanded him to paint sacred art. From this point he devoted his life exclusively to painting and creating works of folk art.

Scholars and art critics have compared his religious work to 19th Century tent-revival posters. His art includes historical figures such as Ronald Reagan, George Washington and Henry Ford as well as visions of heaven and hell, and life on other planets. Finster also painted popular contemporary individuals Marilyn Monroe and Elvis Presley. His drawings of Coca-Cola bottles are probably the most popular of his works. They included slogans, such as "Drink Coke – Drive Home Sober" and "There are no Cokes in Hell" among others.

In 1996 the Coca-Cola Company commissioned Finster to paint an eight foot replica of Coke bottles to represent the United States in an art exhibit for the 1996 Olympic Games in Atlanta. The Athens, Georgia–based alternative rock band, R.E.M., and the Talking Heads

Howard Finster at Paradise Garden

band both commissioned Finster to paint images for the covers of their albums, *Reckoning Stone* in 1984 and *Little Creations* in 1985. The Talking Heads cover won *Rolling Stone Magazine's* award for album cover of the year.

During the late 1980s and 1990, the popularity of Finster's art continued to grow with examples of his art shown at the Library of Congress and the Smithsonian Institute. He made several appearances on television in the United States and other countries including the *Tonight Show* with Johnny Carson. Finster saw the media exposure as an opportunity to preach the gospel. Finster also was the guest of Presidents Reagan and Clinton at the White House.

In December 1995 the High Museum of Art in Atlanta presented an exhibit of his art and treated him to a birthday party. Thereafter he donated some of the Paradise Garden sculptures to the museum to become part of its permanent collections. Finster died on October 22, 2001, of congestive heart failure. By the date of his death he had completed the 46,000 pieces of art.

"Finster's eccentric personality, prolific output, and popular acclaim guaranteed him a place as one of the most celebrated self-taught artists of the 20th Century." Examples of his work are available for purchase from Roots Gallery on the link to his name for varying amounts between $1295 and $1495.

At least three books have been written about the eccentric Howard Finster.

- Bradshaw, Thelma Finster – *Howard Finster: The Early Years.* Birmingham, Ala: Crave Hill Publishers 2001.
- Finster, Howard and Tom Patterson – *Howard Finster, Stranger from Another World: Man of Visions Now On This Earlh*, New York: Abbeville Press, June 1989.
- Peacock, Robert – *Paradise Garden,* San Francisco: Chronicle Books, 1996

In April 2011 Paradise Gardens was added to the National Register of Historic Places. Finster Fest, a celebration of folk art is normally held each year on Memorial Day. Summerville is reached by U.S. Highway 27 S or by taking a ride on one of the Tennessee Valley Railroad Museum excursions from Chattanooga. Check tvrail.com for the train schedule. To reach Paradise Gardens on U.S. 27, travel two blocks south of the Walmart and turn at milepost 13 onto Pine Street. Drive three blocks until the street ends; then turn right. Paradise Gardens will be on the right.

OLIVER HARDY – HARLEM'S COMEDIAN

If you are old enough to remember black and white television and movies, or have heard your parents/grandparents mention the long running "Laurel and Hardy" comedy series, be advised that the heavyset partner Oliver Hardy, was born in Harlem -- Georgia.

Oliver Norvell Hardy was born on January 18, 1892, near the Savannah River down the road from a military installation – Fort Gordon. The town was originally named Saw Dust until the 1860s when the building of a Georgia railroad town took place. Freight trains still travel that route today.

Hardy became one half of the famous comedy team of Laurel and Hardy in the silent film era that lasted from 1927 to 1955. His partner was the pan-faced colleague, Stan Laurel, (Arthur Stanley Jefferson) a native of Ulverston, England, having been born on June 16, 1890.

Together they would revolutionize comedy as they appeared in 107 short feature films and cameo roles. The high point of their successful careers would be the winning of an Academy Award (Oscar) for their short subject entitled "The Music Box" in 1932.

Hardy was the son of a Confederate veteran of the Civil War and had been destined for a military career, but he had opened a movie theater in the neighboring town of Milledgeville, Georgia.

Harlem's water tower features Oliver Hardy

He later would commence his acting career in Jacksonville, Florida, in 1913 after attending the Georgia Military Academy, the Atlanta Conservatory of Music, and the University of Georgia for a short period of time.

After working at the newly established film colony in Florida and performing at various studios on the East Coast, he moved to Hollywood, California, in 1918 and by the mid-1920s was working as an all-purpose comic at the Hal Roach Studios.

Stan Laurel was the son of a British showman and had been raised in British music halls. In 1910 he made a trip to America in a musical comedy troupe which included a fellow performer, Charlie Chaplin. After his initial trip he stayed in the United States touring in vaudeville and performing in small parts in the silent film industry.

Lauren and Hardy first became a duo at the Roach Studios. Their partnership began in 1926. The first time that they performed together in a motion picture was the silent short "The Lucky Dog" in 1921. Their lifelong professional and personal relationship lasted until Oliver died of a massive stroke on August 7, 1957. Stan would die on February 23, 1965, of a heart attack at the age of 74.

In 1981 a film on the lives of the two comedians, Stan and Ollie, staring Steve Coogan as Laurel and John C. Reilly as Hardy was produced. It depicted the twilight years of their careers.

The town of Harlem has not forgotten the famous pacesetters of early comedy as they have established the "Laurel and Hardy Museum of Harlem," 135 N. Louisville Street, Harlem, Georgia 30814-5078. It contains artifacts, memorabilia, and a theatre room to view the many movies that Stan and "Babe" (Hardy's nickname to friends) made together. Admission is free but donations are accepted. Patrons are encouraged to stay and watch a movie or two in which the duo performed. The operating hours are Tuesday – Saturday 10:00 am – 4:00 pm. (706) 556-0401.

The size of the museum limits the size of the exhibits to about 20-25% of the approximately 7000 items donated by friends from around the world. The items are rotated every three months. Visitors describe the museum as, "Clean, well kept – friendly staff and great Laurel and Hardy historical items." A gift shop and opportunity to have your picture taken through life-size cutouts of Stan and Ollie are also available.

A curator is available to answer questions, and each year during the first week of October a music festival takes place.

For a trip to a Southern Harlem, it might be worthwhile.

JACKSON C. PHARRIS – GEORGIA PEARL HARBOR HERO

Jackson C. Pharris is one of several Medal of Honor recipients for valor based on their actions during the Japanese attack on Pearl Harbor on December 7, 1947.

Pharris was born on June 26, 1912 in Columbus, Georgia as the oldest of five children. At the age of 21 he joined the United States Navy on April 25, 1933 and was a gunner on the USS California. After serving on the USS Mississippi he was reassigned back to the California in January 1941. After service at sea the ship reached Pearl Harbor on November 8, 1941.

When the dastardly attack started during the early Sunday morning hours, Pharris was in charge of the ordinance repair party on the third deck of the ship when a torpedo struck under his station. Although stunned and severely injured by the concussion, Pharris on his own initiative set up a hand-supply ammunition train for the ship's anti-aircraft guns.

When the port bulkhead had been torn up from the deck, many crew members were over-come by fumes, and although twice wounded, Pharris, seriously injured, entered flooded compartments and dragged to safety several unconscious shipmates submerged in oil at a substantial risk to his personal safety.

As a result of his courageous action, President Harry S. Truman on June 25, 1948, presented the Medal of Honor for his "conspicuous gallantry and intrepidity" during the Pearl Harbor raid.

Due to the previous injuries he received Pharris was hospitalized at the Naval hospital in Pearl Harbor until March 1942. Ironically he was able to be returned to duty on the USS California which had been repaired and continued to be a part of the Pacific Fleet. Pharris would continue to suffer from lack of oxygen due to oil in his lungs, but he obtained his commission as an officer on July 17, 1942.

Despite continuing medical problems, he returned to duty in June 1943 and later was assigned to the USS Saint Paul, a heavy cruiser in the anticipated invasion of the Japanese mainland.

Although the surrender proclamation had been in effect for five days the ship was attacked by a Japanese kamikaze plane. Pharris directed the crew to take cover, and he assumed control of the anti-aircraft guns which shot down the Zero. His back was broken as a result of the impact of the guns when firing. After receiving medical treatment at a number of naval hospitals, he retired from military service. In May 1948, he was medically retired with the rank of lieutenant commander.

He and his wife Elizabeth and their four children established a residence in Rolling Hills Estates in Los Angeles, California. On October 16, 1966 Pharris collapsed while attending a Congressional Medal of Honor event and died of a heart attack the next day. He was buried in Arlington National Cemetery.

The intrigue and mystery surrounding Jackson Pharris' medals did not end with his death in 1966 at the age of 54. His widow lived until February 14, 2001, and upon her husband's death assumed possession of his medals. Unbeknown to three of her children, her daughter, Janet, placed the multiple medals in a safe deposit box in San Pedro, California. When the three surviving children went through their mother and late sisters possessions after their deaths, they discovered that their father's medals were missing.

After Janet Pharris died, the medals sat in the bank's safety deposit box for three years and then were turned over to the State of California as unclaimed property under state laws. Several years passed, and despite dedicated efforts of the three surviving children, they could not locate the military medals.

Eventually California law would be changed by the legislature to eliminate some of the red tape and to make it easier to return seized property to its rightful owners. When State Controller John Chiang had a news conference, he mentioned some of the odd items which the state has seized over the years. He specifically mentioned a Medal of Honor.

At a ceremony attended by a dozen Pearl Harbor survivors at Coronado Naval Amphibious Base the medal was returned to the Pharris family. Son, Jack Pharris, described his father as a "modest guy" who felt sheepish about receiving the award and often stated that he "believed that plenty of other sailors were every bit as brave as he was that day."

A worthy attitude for one of Georgia's military heroes!

BEFORE MARJORIE – THERE WAS LARRY!

The nationwide controversy over the winner of the 2020 contest in Georgia's 14th Congressional District in the House of Representatives, Marjorie Taylor Greene, doesn't need to be elaborated on further except to confirm that she won almost 75% of the vote as an arch conservative Republican candidate.

Her district starts in Marietta and generally follows Interstate 75 northward covering twelve counties to the Tennessee state line in Catoosa County. In 2016 past president Donald Trump carried the district with the eighth best showing in the nation, and statistics further show that the 14th District is the tenth most Republican district in America.

Retired Congressman Tom Graves served from 2012 – 2020 as the Republican standard bearer. The district has for many years been a conservative district, but it was occupied by Congressman Larry Patton McDonald, a Democrat, in what was formerly the 7th congressional district from 1975-1983. McDonald was a distant relative of General George S. Patton and was born in Atlanta, Georgia on April 1, 1935.

He attended several private and parochial schools as well as a non-denominational high school and also attended Davidson College in North Carolina for two years. He then entered the Emory University School of Medicine in Atlanta at the age of 17. He graduated in 1957 with a medical degree.

McDonald would serve two years as a flight surgeon in the United States Navy stationed in Iceland. He married an Icelandic national and had three children. It was in Iceland that he became concerned about the spread of communism which concern would follow him the rest of his life.

Following his military tour of duty, he returned to Atlanta and resumed his career as an urologist at the McDonald Urology Clinic. His interests in politics would lead to retirement as a practicing physician. He became an avid member of the John Birch Society which further fired his anti-communism belief and became a major theme of his life.

McDonald was an elegant orator and lost to incumbent Congressman John Davis in his first campaign for Congress in 1972 but was elected in 1974. He would serve until his death on September 1, 1983. He defeated Davis on a platform of being opposed to mandatory federal school integration and school busing. He attacked the out-of-state groups who gave his opponent substantial political contributions to support mandatory federal programs that used busing to achieve school integration.

Although he beat Davis in the Democratic primary, a Vietnam War prisoner of war almost beat McDonald as a Republican, indicating a future shift towards the GOP in spite of the fact that the post-Nixon scandal had resulted in the election of 75 new Democrats to Congress. Barely surviving a defeat in the General Election, McDonald would never again be involved in a close election race.

He was an admirer of Senator Joe "Tailgunner" McCarthy, the most vocal anti-communist in the infamous House Committee on Un-American Activities (HUAC.) Larry hoped to be appointed to it when he was elected to Congress, but its heyday in the 1950-1960s had passed, and the committee was in the process of being dissolved.

Larry McDonald was supported by the National Right to Life Committee, Gun Owners of America, and was described by one publication as "the leading anti-communist in America."

He employed the strategy of not often speaking before the microphones/cameras in the House of Representatives while introducing over 150 bills during his tenure in Washington. Instead he used the tactic of inserting material into the Congressional Record.

He would alternatively move to impeach United Nations Ambassador Andrew Young while introducing legislation to place statues of Booker T. Washington and George Washington Carver in the Capitol.

He gained support in the 1980s from Jerry Falwell and the Moral Majority, Senator Jessie Helms of North Carolina, and multi-millionaire conservative financier Nelson Bunker Hunt. In Congress his closest confidant and voting partner was another physician, Dr. Ron Paul of Kentucky, father of the current senator, Dr. Rand Paul.

A series of bizarre incidents kept his name before the public and his high rating in his home congressional district. Many of the ultra-conservative principles he espoused as a Democrat have been adopted by Republican candidates.

Although his brother allegedly told the *Atlanta Constitution* in 1983 that he wore a "bulletproof vest," the record is reportedly silent as to whether he was ever photographed "holding an assault rifle." Perhaps his most outrageous reported advocacy was the suggestion to release the convicted war criminal Rudolph Hess from his decades long imprisonment. According to a report in a local newspaper, he made an alleged suggestion during a political debate that Hess be nominated for the Nobel Peace Prize.

On September 1, 1983, Larry McDonald was a passenger on the Korean Air Lines (KAL) flight to Seoul, South Korea, which was shot down by Russian fighter jets near Sakhalin in the Soviet Union when it allegedly wandered into Soviet air space. All 262 passengers and crew were killed in the incident, which caused an international crisis and also led to all types of conspiracy theories, including one that McDonald was on a spy mission.

Because of bad weather Larry's flight from Atlanta to JFK was diverted to Baltimore and the connecting flight to New York was late, and McDonald missed his connection to South Korea by a few minutes. In a move not typical today, McDonald refused a Pan Am Boeing 747 flight because of the cost to the taxpayers and chose to wait for the next KAL flight two days later. The decision resulted in his death.

In 1998 the Georgia legislature in recognition of McDonald's "service to his district" named the part of I-75 that runs from the Chattahoochee River northward to the Tennessee State line, the Larry McDonald Memorial Highway. Numerous research sources on the world wide web provide lengthy historical facts about the controversial life of the late Congressman from Georgia.

Marjorie Taylor Greene appears to be continuing in a political career reminiscent of Larry McDonald. Whether she will have a section of interstate highway named after her remains in the future?

JOHNNY CASH MEETS WALKER COUNTY SHERIFF RALPH JONES

The turbulent life of country music legend Johnny Cash (February 26, 1932-September 12, 2003) is well documented in song and the written accounts in the news media.

The story of his impoverished youth in Arkansas, honorable military service, rise in his musical career, continued addiction to drugs, and his conversion to Christianity are well contained in his autobiography written in 1975, *Man In Black,* published by Zondervan Publishing Corporation of Grand Rapids, Michigan. It tells a compelling life story of a great talent dealing with the ultimate accomplishments and failures in his personal and musical life that fluctuated between sorrow and happiness.

The period that comes after writing *Man in Black* in 1975 until Cash's death in 2003, only four months after his beloved second wife June Carter Cash's passing, also contains many episodes of sobriety from his drug addiction to amphetamines and barbiturates and subsequent additional relapses from the demons that affected his entire life.

Cash was arrested seven times and was fortunate that during that era law enforcement was not as much affected by media exposure, and his star persona would always help him obtain leniency in the criminal justice system.

In 1957 Cash was introduced to amphetamines (uppers) that allowed him to function at a heightened and unrealistic level of energy. Unfortunately this would also lead to alcohol abuse and consumption of barbiturates (downers) which affected not only his musical performances but his personal life with his family. His wife of twelve years, Vivian, the mother of his three daughters Roseanne, Cindy, and Tara, filed for divorce in 1966, and she was awarded custody of the girls and substantial alimony.

Sheriff Ralph Jones of Walker County, Georgia, was a typical rural county law officer in northwest Georgia. He was friendly to his constituents, tough on hardened criminals, and sympathetic to the locals within his jurisdiction. He served the citizens of Walker County as their highest law enforcement officer in that jurisdiction from January 1, 1969, to December 21, 1984, when he retired.

He was a big fan of Johnny Cash and had followed his career for many years. He owned every record that Cash had produced. He and his wife watched Cash on television and listened to the singer on the radio. Jones was particularly fond of the gospel hymns and claimed that he and his wife were two of the country music star's biggest fans.

Until October, 1967, he had never personally met Johnny Cash, but that meeting would occur under unexpected circumstances. Accounts of Cash's and Jones' first meeting differ in some details, but the description is generally correct.

One of the Walker County deputies had arrested Cash for prowling, public intoxication, and a variety of other charges involving drugs after he had repeatedly banged on the door of a Walker County resident. Cash had allegedly wandered around the county looking for Civil War relics while under the influence of drugs. Another charge was added to the list when Cash allegedly attempted to bribe the arresting deputy, Bobby Edward, with a wad of $100.00 bills. Cash was placed in the Walker County jail where he spent the night.

The first meeting of the country legend star and one of his biggest and loyalest fans did not occur at any musical venue such as the Grand Ole Opry in Nashville. It took place at the ancient jail in Lafayette, Georgia.

In an exercise of law enforcement discretion rarely seen today, Sheriff Jones ordered that the charges against Johnny Cash be thrown out but only after a face to face talk with the superstar wherein he allegedly also gave back Cash's money and the drugs found on his person.

Before releasing him, Jones advised Cash, "Do with your life whatever you want to. Just remember, you've got the free will to kill yourself or save your life," and the sheriff sent him on his way.

Johnny Cash credited Sheriff Jones with being the moving force that turned his life around. He would relapse and often have to go into rehab on other occasions prior to his death in 2003, but he always gave credit to the rural Georgia sheriff for causing him to begin to fight the demons in his life.

On national television shows such as "This Is Your Life," (1971) Cash also gave Sheriff Jones credit for being an influence which may have saved his life. Jones was one of the surprise guests that appeared on the show. In 1970 Cash showed his appreciation by performing a concert in Lafayette which attracted over 12,000 fans in a county of only 8,500 citizens. The $75,000 ($409,793.88 in 2010 dollars) raised at the concert helped to pay off the debt of building Lafayette High School's football stadium and making additional improvements to the school's athletic facilities.

The meeting of the Man in Black and Sheriff Ralph Jones became memorable events in Johnny Cash's life and the law enforcement career of Ralph Jones.

WHO WERE THE GEORGIA WOOL HAT BOYS?

After the Civil War, Southern white men returned to their devastated farms where they were required to perform the duties that were formerly handled by now-freed slaves. The majority of black farm workers left the areas, and the Confederate veterans had to do their own plowing, haying, and picking of cotton and other commodities.

The slaves who toiled in the hot Georgia sun had worn cool, wide-brim straw field hats. The white farmers refused to wear those hats and instead wore sweaty, narrow-brim hats. As they bent over to work the sun would turn their necks red, which led to the creation of the term "redneck."

The "wool hat boys" was the term used to refer to the broad-based populist movement that was critical to the political careers of politicians in the South in the late nineteenth and early twentieth centuries. The term was intended to distinguish white lower and middle class working people from the wealthy "silk coat" plutocrats.

In Georgia the wool hat boys were originally a highly organized and effective political force. Governor Eugene Talmadge, and after him Marvin Griffin, were later beneficiaries of the movement in the 1950's-1960's. Talmadge rose to political power at its crest, and Griffin caught it at the tail end of the era. Rural dominance in state legislatures was ending in the South as the result of the various decisions of the United States Supreme Court in civil rights that made blacks a new political force. The one-man-one-vote decision in 1962 shifted power from the county to the city.

Due to the similarity of the wool hat boys movement and the Democratic Party in Georgia, the former proved to be a short-term phenomenon that became subservient to the progressive movements domination of the Democrats. Due to internal conflicts in the party in the 1880's in Georgia, there were three separate and distinct factions among the farmers' group. Because of the conflicts among the factions, one group proceeded to organize the Populist Party. Genuine interest in populism rose in 1893 when the United States plunged into a devastating Depression.

However, the efforts of the Populist Party leader in the 1894 and 1896 elections to overthrow the Democratic Party in Georgia were unsuccessful. After 1896 the influence of the Populist Party substantially declined until the party remnants gradually disappeared.

The history of the Populist movement and the "Wool Hat Boys" in Georgia is covered extensively in Barton C. Shaw's publication *The Wool Hat Boys: Georgia's Populist Party*. Baton Rouge: Louisiana State University Press (1984). Numerous new and used copies are available on Amazon.com.

SUSAN HAYWARD'S GEORGIA CONNECTION
(JUNE 30, 1917-MARCH 4, 1975)

Although born in the Flat Bush section of Brooklyn, New York, Edythe Marrenner aka Susan Hayward lived in the State of Georgia for a period of about ten years and is buried in the Our Lady of Perpetual Help Cemetery in Carrolton, Georgia.

A talented but highly emotional actress, she started her career as a twenty-year-old fashion model in Hollywood in 1937. She had originally gone to California as one of the hundreds of girls who responded to a national contest to try out for the role of Scarlett O'Hara in *Gone with the Wind* (1939). Although she did not win, her milk white complexion, striking red hair and screen test got her a movie contract.

In October 1941, she was a featured guest at the annual Cotton Ball held at the Memorial Auditorium in Chattanooga on Friday. She also attended the Saturday night Red, White and Blue Soldiers Ball before 2,000 servicemen and their dates, where she gave a short address to the crowd before leaving to catch a flight back to Hollywood.

In her initial movie career, she was relegated to small supporting roles throughout the later 1930's and 1940's. She took acting and voice lessons subsidized by several movie studios for several years. As her acting ability improved, so did the quality of her film roles, and over the course of her acting career, she received five Academy Award nominations. She finally won the Best Actress Award for portraying California death-row inmate Barbara Graham in the highly emotional film *I Want to Live!* in 1958.

Susan received accolades for her acting ability in four previous nominations but lost out to Loretta Young in 1947, Olivia de Havilland in 1949, Shirley Booth in 1952, and Anna Magnani in 1955. The losses led to further disappointments, and she developed a fatalistic attitude thinking that she would never win an Oscar.

Finally in 1958 she achieved her lifelong dream and won as Best Actress. Her portrayal of the female murderer was considered by many movie critics to be one of the finest performances in film history. Susan had several emotional problems which initially arose out of a feeling that she had been neglected by her mother in favor of her older sister, Florence. This would lead to a lifelong grudge towards her mother.

She had other personality traits that may have seemed strange for a Hollywood actress. She did not like socializing with large crowds in the glamour capital of the country, and she projected an image of being aloof, cold, and uneasy. In spite of these characteristics, she was generally held in high esteem by the movie directors that she worked with because her of high standards of professionalism.

Susan loved the outdoors and sport fishing and would become prolific in seeking big fish on one of her three ocean boats. She had a dislike for homosexuals and feminine men and was attracted to men who had displayed very masculine traits. Both of her husband's fit that category. She was first married to actor Jess Barker for a period of ten years. The marriage produced two twin boys in 1945. However the marriage ended in a bitter divorce in 1954. Following the breakup of her marriage she attempted to commit suicide.

In 1957 she married Eaton Chalkey who was a resident of Carrolton, Georgia, and who was a successful rancher and businessman and former FBI agent. Eaton was not a typical husband for a Hollywood movie star, but the couple enjoyed a happy life until he died in January of 1966 of hepatitis. This tragic event sent Susan into another emotional collapse which limited her acting career for several years.

Having lost her husband, she moved to Florida to avoid being reminded of his death by staying in her Georgia home. Prior to his death the couple were baptized into the Catholic faith in December 1964, in Pittsburg, Pennsylvania.

Over the years she had become a two pack a day smoker of cigarettes and a heavy consumer of alcohol. She limited her roles in films to about one performance a year after the death of her husband. The last movie in which she appeared was *The Revenger* in 1972, although she also performed television roles. Throughout her movie career she performed in a total of sixty-four movies.

Her last public appearance was at the Academy Awards telecast in 1974 to present the Best Actress Award. She was very ill and had to be assisted by fellow actor Charleston Heston, but she made it through the ceremony where she was cheered loudly by the audience.

Her ties to the State of Georgia are permanent as she was buried in the church cemetery of the Our Lady of Perpetual Help Roman Catholic Church in Carrolton adjacent to the funeral plot of her second husband, Eaton Chalkey.

LEO FRANK – ATLANTA'S MURDER VICTIM

Until the "Atlanta Wayne William Child Murders" between July 1979 and May 1981, involving the deaths of 28 young children, adolescents, and adults, the most famous murder case in Georgia was that of Leo Frank.

Every lawyer and non-lawyer should review some of the various articles on this landmark case to ascertain what happened in a case totally absorbed with Antisemitism, abusive and prejudicial news coverage, prosecutorial misconduct by law enforcement and a district attorney, jury and witness tampering, use of perjured testimony, forced confessions, and many other violations of constitutional rights. Fortunately our courts now address these violations, but such restraints were totally lacking in 1913-1915.

In 1913 Frank was convicted of the murder of a fellow employee, Mary Phagan, in Atlanta, Georgia. Both Frank and his alleged murder victim were employed at the National Pencil Company.

Frank was born to a Jewish-American family in Cuero, Texas, on April 17, 1884, and at an early age his family moved to New York where he attended Cornell University and earned a degree in mechanical engineering before moving to Atlanta in 1910.

The victim, Mary Phagan was employed at the pencil factory at the hourly wage of ten cents. She was strangled on April 26, 1913, and her body was found the next day in the plant's cellar.

Initially three individuals: Leo Frank, the night watchman; Newt Lee; and Jim Conley, a black janitor, were all suspects and jailed. Lee would be dismissed as the potential killer, and Conley would be the star witness who testified as an alleged accomplice of Frank in the murder. Despite defense efforts to paint Conley as the actual murderer, their efforts were unsuccessful, and Frank was convicted and sentenced to death.

What followed the trial were various hearings and appeals through appellant courts that ended in the United States Supreme Court decision of Frank v. Mangrum, 273 U.S. 309 (1915.) The High Court, by a vote of 7-2, affirmed Frank's conviction and sentence on the grounds that his lawyer had failed to raise the issue timely of whether his client's constitutional right to be present when he was sentenced in absence in the Judge's chambers because of potential mob violence, was violated.

In an earlier 142 page opinion by the Georgia Supreme Court on February 17, 1914, it had rejected the argument on the same issue by a 4-2 vote.

Upon reviewing the facts of the case, beginning with the murder of Mary Phagan on April 26, 1913, and concluding that the lynching of Leo Frank on August 17, 1915 was unlawful, a reader has to be appalled at the complete breakdown and collapse of the justice system in Atlanta.

History has belatedly changed the results of this horrendous black mark on the scales of justice by a posthumous pardon of Leo Frank in 1986 by the Georgia State Board of Pardons and Paroles, although it failed to completely clear Frank of the crime in a totally inadequate gesture based on a complete abandonment of the principles of "right to a fair trial' and "due process of law."

The final destructive step in this breakdown of justice was when Frank was kidnapped from the Milledgeville State Prison where he had been taken for protection, and when a gang of lynchers summarily executed him in a public display in Marietta.

One of the few acts of courage in the case was when Georgia Governor John M. Slaton in 1915 commuted Frank's sentence from capital punishment to life imprisonment after a full examination of the trial testimony as well as new exonerating evidence produced afterwards. Slaton's actions were the basis for the illegal vigilante action that led to Frank's lynching on August 17.

A good starting point for a review of the facts, circumstances, and various court rulings would be a review of the lengthy Georgia Supreme Court decision of Frank v. State of Georgia, 114 GA. 243 (1914), the U.S. Supreme Court decision of Frank v. Mangum 273 U.S. 309 (1915) and the twenty-four page summary of the case in Wikipedia under the name of Leo Frank. Any further interest in this case can be satisfied by examination of the various sources listed in the chronology at the end of the article.

Hopefully such a sensational travesty of our legal justice system will never occur again.

RUBE GARLAND – ATLANTA ADVOCATE
(1902 – 1982)

Reuben A. Garland, Sr. (Rube) was a fifth-generation lawyer from Atlanta who acquired a local, state, and national reputation as a trial lawyer for defendants in criminal cases. Rube practiced law for over sixty years and reportedly handled over 500 murder cases. He only lost one decision that resulted in the death penalty against his client.

During the 1920s – 1960s he was considered by many to be the South's most successful and flamboyant defender of the accused. He was the predecessor to the late Bobby Lee Cook as a Georgia courtroom attorney and was just as colorful and controversial. According to reports, he sometimes appeared in court in a sky-blue silk suit or a tuxedo with tails, twirling a walking stick and using theatrical tactics.

He once held the record for the largest civil damages award by a jury and was recognized as a premier criminal defense lawyer. Never quitting, he fought for his clients and did not hesitate from vigorously attacking witnesses, prosecutors, or even judges if he felt they were infringing on his efforts to secure an acquittal on his cleats' behalf.

Rules of lawyer conduct were different and more lenient in his many years of practice. Rube was found guilty of contempt of court on several occasions. In that era, paying a fine was usually the punishment rather than facing discipline that could result in suspending their law license or disbarment by the state supreme court upon recommendation of a legislative judicially-created bureaucracy.

When he overstepped the limits of propriety before the court he was often lightly punished. However, one Judge in the Superior Court in the Atlanta Circuit did not take kindly to Mr. Garland's remarks during a trial on January 23, 1959. He stated that the attorney, "Willfully made numerous inflammatory and prejudicial statements in the presence of the jury and that Reuben A. Garland having made numerous contemptuous and prejudicial remarks to the court, and the said

Garland having willfully suggested answers and information to witnesses while testifying after specific instructions from the court not to do so... the conduct was intended by said Garland to be contemptuous of the court, and said conduct did interfere with the lawful administration of justice."

After further ruling that Rube's conduct occurred in open court and in the presence of the court (and jury) the trial judge held the lawyer in contempt for three incidents and sentenced him to twenty days in the Fulton county jail, with two sentences running consecutive to another, for a total period of incarceration of forty days. A third contempt of another twenty days was allowed to run concurrently with the first two sentences. The history of said case is contained in the Georgia Supreme Court reported decision of Garland v. Tanksley 99 Ga. App. 201 107 S.E. 866 (1959).

Rube's son, Attorney Eddie Garland, remembers two specific incidents during his dad's incarceration. While playing in a football game in junior high school, he looked over at the sidelines and saw and heard his father cheering his team while being accompanied by a Fulton County deputy sheriff. A photo appeared on the front page of one of the Atlanta newspapers showing Rube's butler entering the Fulton jail carrying a covered silver tray containing daily meals for the lawyer.

Although the case created much interest in the legal profession, it was not the only time Rube was held in contempt for his courtroom antics in defense of his client. Once after being cited for misconduct and fined $10, Garland allegedly pulled out a $100 bill and told the court that he was, "Paying for nine more contempt actions in advance."

Rube Garland can also be remembered for defending black defendants at a time when many other lawyers would not do so in the segregated South.

At the age of 68, he unexpectedly went to Vietnam to represent a black soldier before an all-white panel of officers in a court martial case alleging that the Marine Lance Corporal had thrown a hand grenade into an enlisted service club outside DaNang, killing one man and injuring 63 others. After a trial that was often interrupted by rocket attacks, the young man was acquitted primarily as the result of Garland's aggressive cross-examination of the star government accuser, alleged co-conspirator and co-perpetrator of the crime.

Rube Garland is alleged to have had great respect for fair and honest judges but had none for a judge who he thought was either dishonest or abusing his client's right to a fair trial. One of the most daring tactics employed by him was when he believed that one of the Superior Court judges in Atlanta was partly responsible for a disbarment proceeding against him that would jeopardize his law license and prevent him from engaging in his chosen profession.

There were eleven judges in the Atlanta judicial circuit, and it was known that there were severe political differences among some of them. Garland subpoenaed all of the judicial officers and put several on the witness stand to testify that they would not believe under oath "some of the judicial officers that were responsible for the efforts to disbar Rube Garland."

The legacy of the Garland law firm for providing outstanding criminal and civil representation was maintained when Edward (Eddie) T. M. Garland began practice in 1963. It continues with the entry of seventh generation attorney John A. Garland into the firm in 2004.

The rules governing the practice of law and conduct of lawyers are quite different from the days of Rube Garland's practice, but his dedication to the principle that an attorney's first loyalty is to his client is not.

WERE THE WRIGHT BROTHERS FIRST? (MICAJAH CLARK DYER)

Historians across the country and particularly in North Carolina traditionally credit the brother team of Orville and Wilbur Wright with being the first to invent a flying machine for manual flight.

However, folks in Blairsville, Georgia, have a pretty strong argument that a resident of the community in Union County may have preceded the more famous brothers by about twenty-nine years.

Micajah Clark Dyer was born in Pendleton District, South Carolina on July 13, 1822 and moved to Union County while he was still a young boy. He would die on January 26, 1891.

Although Clark had only a seventh-grade education, he had a creative mind and invented several gadgets and procedures. He built and operated a gristmill from about 1850 to 1890 grinding grain for his family and neighbors on several hundred acres in the remote area of Choestoe Valley.

On September 1, 1874, Dyer received Patent No. 154,654 titled "Apparatus for Navigating the Air" from the United States Patent Office. It was also placed in Class 244 for "Aeronautics and Astronautics" and in Subclass 28 for "Airships with Beating Wings Sustained."

Conflicting reports exist as to whether Clark's experiments and test flights ever received any local attention or notoriety. Some stories claim that there were no local newspapers in existence that mentioned his invention, but it was also stated that it was reported in dozens of newspapers in other towns across the U.S. and perhaps also in foreign countries. Eyewitness accounts from family, neighbors and friends document him flying off of the side of Rattlesnake Mountain in his flying machine, and such accounts were published in the *Gainesville Eagle* in Georgia as well as in the *St. Louis Globe Democrat*.

The editor and publisher of the *Eagle* was John G. Redwine. One of the rumors that exists is that after Clark's death in 1891 at the age of sixty eight, his widow, Morena Ownbey Dyer, sold the flying machine and its design to the Redwine Brothers who were wealthy manufacturers in Atlanta, Georgia.

Whether they were related to John Redwine or were ever told about any article in the *Gainesville Eagle* has never been disclosed in published accounts. If there is a family connection between the local and Atlanta Redwine families, it would be strong circumstantial evidence that there was a potential profit motive involved.

Further supporting evidence is that the Wright Brothers supposedly attempted to purchase every existing patent in the field of aviation that was related to the efforts by humans to fly, but no direct proof exists as to a sale of Clark's patent to the Wright brothers.

Local corroborative proof of Clark Dyer's testimony was also available. A neighbor Francis M. Swain and an uncle, M. C. Dyer, Jr. on February 16, 1874, were witnesses on the patent documents that were filed on June 10, 1874, and approved for entry on September 1, 1874, by the government office.

Clark Dyer was very protective of his flying machine and allegedly kept it under lock and key in a barn. He did not let skeptics in on his experiments in his workshop.

Other witnesses who claimed to have actually seen the invention were Clark's grandson, Johnny Wimpey, a cousin Herschel A. Dyer, and a preachers son, James Washington Lance. Micajah Dyer built a ramp on Rattlesnake Mountain where he allegedly flew in a full-size model with foot controls and a steering device.

When accusations arose as to the sanity of Clark Dyer, a neighbor James M. Rich came to his defense in a letter to the editor of the *Athens Banner – Watchman* on April 28, 1885. Rich exclaimed "He (Dyer) is not crazed, but is dead earnest, and confidently believes that he has solved the problem of aerial navigation." However, it was suggested by a Dr. Thomas Fitzgerald Green who ran the state insane asylum at Milledgeville, Georgia, and who stated in an early article, "The institution may just as well get a room for brother Dyer. If he doesn't break his neck during his first soar, he will certainly land at Milledgeville!!"

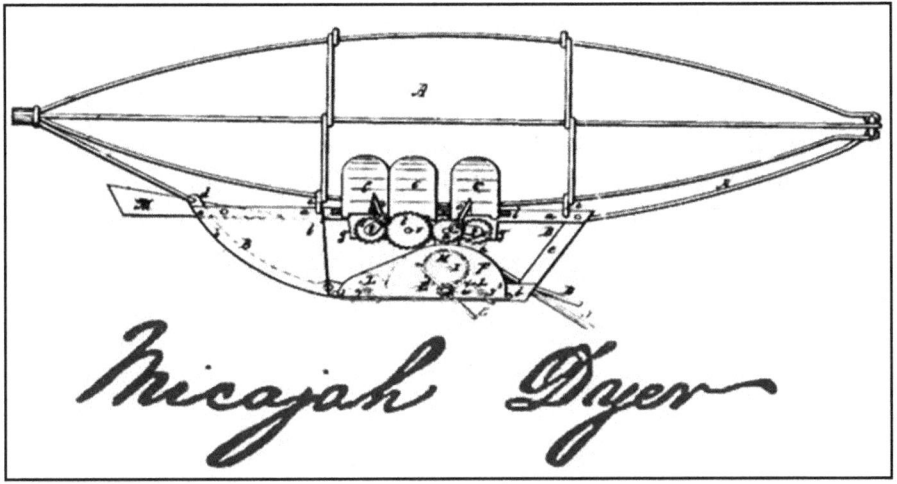

Patent drawing of Micajah Dyer's flying machine

The legend and rumors go on through several sources:

1) His great great granddaughter, Sylvia Dyer Turnage, is an author and has written two published books on the 1874 historical event in *Clark Dyer's Remarkable Flying Machine* (2015) and *Flying off Rattlesnake Mountain* (2017) which are non-fiction accounts of Clark Dyer's efforts.

2) Eyewitness statements of relatives and neighbors who actually viewed some aspect of Dyer's successfully attempts to launch his aircraft or of its existence

3) He did file for and registered a patent of his invention on September 1, 1874. The patent was found in 2004.

4) Numerous area and national newspaper articles reported the status of his work.

5) In 2006, Jack Allen, a retired Delta Airlines Machinist, built a to-scale model with the plans of Dyers machine which was donated to the Union County Historical Society in Blairsville, Georgia. The so-called flying ship has been described as a "small boat under a tube-shaped balloon."

6) Further interest in Micajah Clark Dyer has been perpetuated by a website at www.MicajahClarkDyer.org and also a YouTube video under his name or that of Sylvia Dyer Turnage.

7) He is recognized on a special highway sign near Blairsville, Georgia, designating the road as Micajah Clark Dyer Parkway, Pioneer Aviator, 1822-1891.

Family efforts continue to have him recognized as "Georgia's Pioneer Aviator." His new tombstone in Old Choestoe Cemetery in Choestoe, Union County, Georgia, was placed in 2010 and was erected by "Monies contributed by the Micajah Clark Dyer Foundation, Inc. and relatives and friends to commemorate his contribution to aviation."

BEN EPPS
THE FATHER OF AVIATION IN GEORGIA
(1888-1937)

Although the recognition of the Wright Brothers' short flight at Kitty Hawk, North Carolina, in 1903 is often disputed as to whether they were the first aviators in America or throughout the world, there is little dispute as to who was the "Father of Aviation" in the State of Georgia.

Although there is an argument in support of Micajah Clark Dyer who obtained a patent for his "Apparatus for Navigating the Air" in 1874, it was more like a glider and did not contain a motor. Dyer's story is told in a 2017 publication *Flying off Rattlesnake Mountain* by relative and author Sylvia Dyer Turnage who also named Dyer as "Georgia's Pioneer Aviator."

Ben Epps was born in Oconee, Georgia, on February 28, 1888. He admired the accomplishments of the Wright Brothers while he was a young boy, and he was an inventor who developed a motor driven heavier-than-air flying machine.

Epps was one of ten children and his family moved to Clarke County (Athens) where he attended the local schools. Although he briefly attended the Georgia Institute of Technology, he did not graduate but returned to his hometown to start an electrical contractor business. He also operated the first automobile repair garage in Athens.

While only nineteen years old, he built and flew his first airplane in an open field in his hometown. His initial craft differed from Orville and Wilbur Wright's in that he operated the plane from sitting upright in a buggy seat, whereas the Wright brothers flying machine was flown by lying in a prone position on one of the crafts double wings.

His original flying tactics included the use of bicycle wheels on the bottom of his monoplane, and he used a hill as a runway rather than a takeoff rail used by the Wrights' plane. Similar to their first flight,

Epps' initial successful effort was only about one hundred yards long and only reached an altitude of approximately fifty feet.

Although his oversized craft was not preserved, a replica of his later invention, the "Epps 1912 Monoplane" has been saved and is on display at the Museum of Aviation in Warner Robbins, Georgia.

Epps was not only a prolific flyer he was also a productive father of ten children which was sufficient to exempt him from World War I during the 1917-1918 period of combat. Although not serving in the military, after 1919 he purchased used army surplus airplanes and befriended many wartime flyers such as L. Monte Rolfe. They would join together to form the Rolfe-Epps Flying Service in Athens. The service provided aerial photography, passenger sightseeing trips, and flying lessons to Georgia's first generation of pilots.

The first civilian airport in the state was located three miles from Athens on land rented from Clarke County. Ben's memory is today kept alive by the land being the site of Athens – Ben Epps Airport which he opened in 1917. It is mostly used by private pilots. The University of Georgia athletic teams transported the Bulldog squads to contests around the South. Until 2015, when a six hundred foot runway extension project was completed, the passenger space and available seats needed for the football squad precluded the use of the airport.

Epps continued to build experimental aircraft and in 1925 produced his light monoplane which was a single-seat aircraft. Although he lacked the financial resources to mass produce the monoplane, it was an example of how flying could be made available to the average citizen, and his work helped inspire William Piper to develop his famous Piper Cub in 1931.

Epps love of flying was passed down to his children and many others. His eldest son, Ben Epps, Jr., at age thirteen became at that time in aviation history the youngest pilot to solo and was invited by President Herbert Hoover to make an appearance at the White House in Washington, D.C. As a result, the father and son team became popular "barn storming" participants in stunt flying and air races in the State of Georgia.

Unfortunately, Ben Epps, Sr. died in an airplane crash in a test flight near Athens in 1937. However, the family tradition of flying was carried on by Ben, Jr. who joined the U.S. Army Air Corps. In World War II, he successfully flew C-46 cargo carrier planes over the Himalayan Mountains (The Hump) to provided needed supplies to the legendary "Flying Tigers" in China, Burma, and India.

When the Georgia Aviation Hall of Fame was created in 1989, Ben, Sr. was inducted as a charter member. His selection into the prestigious flying fraternity was followed by Ben, Jr. being enshrined in the Hall in 1994.

The family tradition of being involved in aviation continued when youngest son, Pat set up a fixed base operation (FBO) at DeKalb Peachtree Airport in Atlanta, Georgia.

Other documentation of the life of Ben Epps, Sr. is available in a film titled "Ben Epps: The Legacy of Georgia's First aviator" by William J. Evelyn and Dick Mendenhall (Athens, University of Georgia, 2001) and in an article in the *New Georgia Encyclopedia*, "Ben Epps (1988-1937)" written by Hudson, Paul S. on July 13, 2018, and placed on the world wide web on November 6, 2020.

Although he only lived a short life of forty-nine years, Ben Epps and his family have made significant contributions to the field of Aviation in the State of Georgia.

PEERLESS WOOLEN MILLS, ROSSVILLE, GEORGIA

What was once an intricate part of the thriving northwest Georgia community at Rossville as its main anchor, the Peerless Woolen Mills is now just a shadow of past days of full employment and operation as a prosperous business.

In 1905 after the city of Rossville had been incorporated, the Peerless Woolen Mills operated from 1905-1980. The plant was owned by John L. Hutcheson, Sr., and his son, John L. Hutcheson, Jr. Other purchasers have tried to operate the facility in various capacities, but ownership has now reverted to the Hutcheson family that owns it as the Rossville Development Corporation. The decline of the American textile industry, as well as a devastating fire in 1967, hampered efforts to maintain the facility.

The plant was recognized as one of the world's largest woolen mills. Located on 27 acres of land, it included a full-sized gymnasium that accommodated the mill's semi-pro basketball team in the Southern Textile League. They participated against teams in the various textile plants throughout the South. Minor league baseball players such as the Chattanooga Lookouts' Junior Wooten and others played on the squads to stay in shape during the winter. The league existed from 1921 to 1997. During that period, the Woolens in the 1950's also played the Harlem Globetrotters several times. Walt Lauter, Sr., was a legendary coach and athletic director and oversaw the entire sports program at Peerless.

During this era, the Rossville High School Bulldogs benefited substantially from the favorable viewpoint of the Hutcheson's towards employees who had sons that were good athletes. It was commonly known that, "The more sports that an employee or their son played the better your job at Peerless." In reality it became a fact.

Besides Lauter, former Chattanooga Central and Georgia Tech athlete, Bob McCoy, worked in management and was always looking for athletically talented offspring when employment of a parent was being considered. Lauer also obtained summer employment for many athletes from Rossville High School at the north Georgia amusement park, Lake Winnepesaukah. This helped Rossville High School have outstanding athletic programs and they won numerous games competing against schools with student enrollments much larger than Rossville.

The Little League program in Rossville that played in the all-white Dixie Little Boys League also contributed to the success in sports. In 1961 the World Series was held on Lookout Mountain, Tennessee, at Senter Field. Eight teams representing seven southern states competed for the title.

With a roster of future Southeastern Conference football players, and minor league baseball players, Rossville came out of the losers bracket to claim the championship trophy. Bobby Scott, Ricky Buff, Denny Painter, Ken McGregor, and others participated in various sports past their Dixie Little League careers. Georgia Tech All American Pete Brown was one of the many All State players from Rossville that performed in college. Brown later played in the National Football League with the San Francisco 49ers. Bobby Scott, a Tennessee graduate, spent eleven seasons with the New Orleans Saints.

The plant's fast pitch softball team competed in the top league in Chattanooga over the years. The league included Combustion, Chattanooga Gas, DuPont, Toyota, and others. Former All World player, Jim Ellis, was with the Clearwater Bombers when they won nine world fast-pitch softball titles. He moved to Rossville to be recreation director under Lauter at Peerless.

It is ironic that the leading public high school in Chattanooga in athletics at that time was Chattanooga Central, and although Rossville and Central won numerous state championships in football, the only contests that the two powerhouses competed in against each other were basketball and baseball.

The crumbling and deteriorating plant in Rossville which was once the home of the Peerless Woolen Mills lies silent. Only aging survivors can share the glory days and excitement that brought unity to the closely knit community in Rossville where almost all of its citizens were directly or indirectly involved with the plant throughout the years.

The plant is now closed and only memories of the past victories on the athletic field of both Peerless and Rossville High squads remain vivid and alive in the minds of the players and spectators who had the privilege to be part of the once-vibrant Rossville community.

Local Rossville historian Larry Rose expresses his viewpoint, "The whole area was setup around that mill. Just about everyone in Rossville worked there at one time or another."

At one time the Personality Shop and the La Dean Shop were popular outlets for the women of northwest Georgia and also served many customers from Lookout Mountain and Chattanooga.

A bowling alley, miniature golf course, and movie theater also provided an additional source of recreation for Rossville's residents. One of the few remaining original business is the iconic Roy's Diner which has remained open in spite of several turbulent times. Walter Woods Supply is another entity that has survived.

Rossville Boulevard in Tennessee and going into Rossville across the Georgia state line was a thriving commercial area which was known as the original "automotive row."

Deerings Drive Inn and Big Mike's Barbecue (sign of the Dancing Pig) and the Teridon Restaurant were all popular dining spots that are now long gone.

Hopefully Rossville will someday enjoy the rejuvenation that Chattanooga is presently undergoing.

PEERLESS MILLERS BASEBALL HISTORY

Ever since the opening of the Peerless Woolen Mill by John L. Hutcheson, Sr. in 1905, the plant has always had superb athletic programs both in and outside the plant in basketball, softball and baseball with players using facilities that were superior to many other playing fields or gymnasiums.

Prior to the 1950s, when television changed the practice of many minor league teams from Triple A through AA, A, B, C and D in classifications, existence in small towns as part of the national past time thrived in many communities.

Peerless "Millers" were very active in the 1930s – 1940s and fielded teams that played in the Amateur World Series of the American Baseball Congress. Each year the series would rotate between Battle Creek, Michigan, and Wichita, Kansas.

Eddie Koger's wife's grandfather, Lester "Son" Jarnaigan, was the Millers starting catcher, and her great uncle "Red" Bevis was the team's third baseman during the heydays of the 1930s. Kroger has provided much history of the Millers. The Millers were the perennial champions in the Tennessee-Georgia amateur league and won the title in 1932 and 1933.

In 1935 the team played in the Wichita, Kansas, semi-pro tournament and won four games while losing two in double elimination. According to notes kept by Red Bevis, the tournament was won by the Bismarck, North Dakota, team whose star pitcher was the future Hall-of-Fame pitcher, Satchel Paige, who struck out 60 batters and was selected as an All American. He also was paid $1,000.

Millers' pitcher Buford "Lefty" Denton was also selected for the elite squad. Lefty Denton was considered the premier pitcher in the area for Peerless and had played professional baseball before he got homesick and returned to East Ridge in 1934 and started playing for Peerless. In 1939 the team finished third in the national tournament, and to show the strength of semi-pro baseball, it was reported that there were 36,000 teams through the country competing for the right to play in the national tournament.

Lefty Denton and Red Bevis were once again selected to the first class All-American team. Pick-up players, right fielder Cleve Barrett, and catcher Samuel Case were chosen for the second team. The legendary Walt Lauter was the business-manager and future Rossville mayor and politician. Paul Ellis was a young score keeper.

Another outstanding pitcher was "Preach" Baker, who turned down the requests of Chattanooga Lookout owner Joe Engel to become a professional ballplayer. However, the young player preferred to stay close to his Rock Springs, Georgia, home and chose to play for the Millers.

In 1939 Opening Day was a big event at the Peerless Field with a band playing before thousands of fans and John S. Hutcheson, Jr. throwing out its first ball to his father, John Hutcheson, Sr. Montgomery Montague served as catcher.

Rossville and Peerless were not the only communities that provided top notch amateur baseball teams. The Chickamauga Bleachery, North Chattanooga, East Lake, etc. all had teams with outstanding talent such as future Central High geometry teacher and former professional ballplayer Willard Millsaps, and Ty Coppinger on the Soddy-Daisy team. Other players on the 1939 Millers were Duncan Doty, "Doc" Reavely, Norman Wood, C. L. Billings, Warren Coleman, Lee Settles, "Lonesome" Burch, Jeff Park, Cecil Fowler, Clyde Roberts and J. D. Morton.

Before television, the Peerless Millers were just one part of the nationwide phenomenon known as amateur and semi-pro baseball.

PEERLESS CLIPPER WWII AIRCRAFT CAPTAIN LAURENCE SIES

During World War II it was a common practice to have some type of insignia or saying on the nose of a bomber that reflected some correlation to a hometown or person of the crew.

The Peerless Clipper was one of those aircraft and was purchased as a result of War Bond sales by the Peerless Woolen Mills of Rossville, Georgia, across the state line near Chattanooga, Tennessee. It was a B-24 bomber in the 449 Bomb Group 717, Bomb Squadron. On July 3, 1942, Laurence Durwood Sies graduated from training as an Aviation Cadet and was designated as a pilot in the Army Air Force. The Peerless Clipper was initially assigned to the crew of Chattanooga native, Sies, who operated Sies Electric Company in Chattanooga on 11th Street after the war until his death.

According to his daughter, Katie Henderson, Sies flew fifty-two missions during the war. Twenty-five missions were the normal limit before being transferred to another plane.

The plane was lost on April 2, 1944 over Steyr, Austria, located in the Austrian federal state of Upper Austria. The aircraft flew into a mid-air collision resulting from a rocket attack by Lufwaffe fighters which shot down two other bombers, "Miss Behavin" and "Superstitious Al-o-ysius." The plane then was piloted by 1st Lt. Jake Kury and all eleven members of his crew perished. Only one man survived out of the 31 men flying in the three planes.

Sies would survive the war and raise four daughters. He lost his rank when he flew under the Market Street Bridge in a P51 Mustang on a lark. He moved up the ranks from 2nd Lt. to Major, but as a result of his under the bridge caper, was demoted back to Captain.

According to his son-in-law, Dave Pope, who married Sies youngest daughter, Laura, after serving his 25 missions on the Peerless Clipper, Sies transferred to the O.S.S. which was the predecessor to the present-day CIA. He flew a B-24 bomber at night in an aircraft that had no numbers and was painted black.

The plane's duties including dropping money, propaganda pamphlets and French Nationals of the resistance fighters in occupied France who would be parachuted into their native country.

For his military service, Sies was awarded several decorations while serving in the Air Force. They included the Distinguished Flying Cross American, Distinguished Service Cross, Distinguished Cross France, Silver Star Croix DeGuerre, American Theater Metal, Distinguished Service Medal, European Theater Metal and others.

Another story about a Chattanooga young man and his Rossville Peerless Woolen Mill airplane that is part of the military legacy of our community.

OLD STONE CHURCH MUSEUM – RINGGOLD, GEORGIA

Traveling south from Chattanooga on I-75, interested Southern historians should take a detour at exit 345, turn left on Highway 41 across the bridge and travel about ¾ miles to the site of the Old Stone Church Museum.

In 1837 settlers in the area organized the Chickamauga Presbyterian Church and originally built a small log cabin in which to worship. This was before the Cherokee Indians were removed from the area.

In 1849 the congregation decided to build a new church. Using rock from nearby Taylor Ridge and Stubblefield Farm in Catoosa-Walker County, the new building was completed in 1850. Over the years the structure has been used in several capacities.

Following the defeat of the Confederates at Missionary Ridge in Chattanooga and their retreat towards Atlanta, the Battle of Ringgold Gap on November 27, 1863, took place. Union General Joseph Hooker encountered rebel General Patrick Cleburne, and a battle took place north of the church. Subsequently, Cleburne used the church as a hospital for his wounded, and after he withdrew to the south, Union officers used the church as a stable. Blood stains remain on the wooden floor of the building from treatment of the injured and dying soldiers.

During the reorganization of the Presbyterian Church in 1912, a new church was formed under the name of Chickamauga Presbyterian Church, and it was requested that the church change its name from Chickamauga Presbyterian Church to Stone Church. Around 1920 the church was sold to a Methodist denomination which maintained it for several years until around 1935.

After that the church sat empty until the Catoosa County Historical Association took control of the building in the 1950's. A descendant member of the original congregation, R.C. Magill, expressed his concern about the sale of the building to private speculators and stated, "It was to be used as a roadhouse."

Several different church orders occupied the little church over the years, and it eventually became a mission church for Highland Park Baptist in Chattanooga under the leadership of Dr. Lee Robertson. He was the founder of Tennessee Temple University, and numerous divinity students practiced preaching at Old Stone Church.

Around 1983 the property was purchased by three individuals who gave the property to the North Georgia Methodist Episcopal Church Conference.

In 1995 it was proposed that Highland Park Baptist Church was going to sell the facility to a furniture company. However when it was learned that Highland Park only owned one of approximately twelve shares, the remaining heirs gave their shares to the Catoosa County Historical Society (CCHS). With the help of the State of Georgia and Catoosa County governments, the remaining shares were purchased from Highland Park.

Since 1996 CCHS has attempted to restore the building to as near as its 1880's condition as possible. The property has been updated without infringing upon the requirements of the National Register of Historic Places where it was protected in 1979. The building serves as a museum with numerous items pertaining to the history of the area both before and after the Civil War. Included are the original alter and church pews.

When I-75 was being built through Ringgold Gap, remnants of an old Cherokee village was found. Archaeologists were called in to catalog the site, and the remains of the village were moved to the church to be stored. They are on display in the museum along with many other articles of historical importance.

According to authorities, the singing of the traditional Southern gospel hymn, "Leaning on the Everlasting Arms," written by A.J. Showalter, was first performed at the Old Stone Church.

A publication, *History in Catoosa County* by retired United States Army Major William H. Clark, first published in 1972, devotes a chapter on the Old Stone Church Museum and describes many historical facts about the Ringgold-Catoosa County area. Its third printing occurred in 2012, and copies can be obtained at the church museum.

It contains references and chapters pertaining to the early days of the Cherokee Indians in the county in the 1700's through the Civil War Battles of Ringgold in 1863.

Further information can be obtained by calling (706) 935-5232 or searching on the internet for "Old Stone Church Museum." It is handicap accessible through a separate entrance; admission is free, and musical entertainment is frequently provided by churches and other groups.

A side trip off busy I-75 will be worth the effort for any students of the history of this remarkable structure and the historical area of Ringgold-Catoosa County.

WALKER COUNTY'S FANTASTIC PIT

One of northwest Georgia's best kept secrets in Walker County is the spectacular Fantastic Pit in the secluded Pigeon Mountain area with its rich history including federal troops camping on it prior to the Battle of Chickamauga in the Civil War in September 1863.

The pit is located in Ellison's Cave and is alleged to be the deepest pit cave in the continental United States with a drop of 586 feet (179 meters.) In comparison the vertical shaft is almost twice the size of the State of Liberty and is almost as tall as the Seattle Space Needle, but it is a natural phenomenon. Ellison Cave is the 12th deepest cave in the United States and stretches for about 12 miles in length with a total vertical descent that contains, not only the Fantastic Pit, but others as well. The cave system's unobstructed underground pits enhance the image of the cave as a truly special, spectacular, and dangerous area.

Fantastic Pit is the deepest, but on the opposite side of the cave is Incredible Pit which also has an unobstructed depth of 440 feet. Names have been given to the other shorter depths such as Smokey I (500 feet), Smokey II (262 feet), The Warm-up Pit (125 feet) and a few other shorter pits. All involve an element of danger but also provide an amazing cave system that has been formed through soluble limestone rock formations over millions of years.

The cavernous area has not been commercially developed like Ruby Falls on Lookout Mountain, Tennessee, and should not be visited by inexperienced cavers (spelunkers) who are novices in the sport.

The end result of this unique area is "a dark, echoing and labyrinthine system with seven different routes to the cave floor and plenty of horizontal passages."

Cavers have to initially descend by the shorter Warm Up Pit which presents a degree of difficult challenge of its own. Going lower, there is a cramped space called the Attic which is at the top of the Fantastic Pit. It is from this location that brave and experienced spelunkers can descend into the gigantic pit.

View of Fantastic Pit from the bottom. Photo by Adam Haydock.

Aspiring and curious visitors are warned that entering Ellison's Cave is fraught with dangers that have in the past resulted in the deaths of at least three cavers who became entangled in their ropes while descending, became stuck, and died from hypothermia from the icy temperatures.

Extensive training and experience of the single rope technique in wet conditions and heavy ropes are absolutely essential. Being properly prepared with the right equipment and proper clothing is mandatory before any brave-hearted souls tackle the beautiful but deadly terrain.

A simple warning is given in a website simply entitled "Fantastic Pit – Walker County, Georgia", which includes a series of photos by Adam Haydock. "This is an advanced cave system and therefore is not the proper place for beginner cavers and certainly non-cavers. One has to have extensive vertical caving experience to 'tour the cave'."

However, in spite of its dangerous features, Fantastic Pit is still recognized as one of the "7 Stone Spectacles in Georgia" in the "50 States of Wonder" website.

DURHAM GEORGIA COAL MINES

Durham is an unincorporated community in Walker County, Georgia, that is probably unknown to the majority of the public except for descendants of the miners and families that worked in the mines. Durham was first called Pittsburgh like so many other towns that intended to simulate the big steel metropolis in Pennsylvania. The name of the community changed to Durham after the mining area on Lookout Mountain was purchased by the Durham Iron and Coal Company.

Originally the Cherokee Indians lived in this area but were driven out on the Trial of Tears in 1830. This allowed industrialists to come into the rich coal mining region and to develop the resources. Black convicts provided much of the labor to extract the coal from the mines that had begun operating before the Civil War. When the mines were opened in 1891, foremen were hired to oversee the convicts. The prisoners lived in barracks and were kept under heavy guard night and day.

The first load of coal from the Durham mines went on exhibition at the Georgia depot yard in Chattanooga on January 5, 1892. Originally the coal going to Chattanooga was hauled from the mines by mule-pulled wagons to a winding precarious railroad, the Chattanooga Southern Railroad, constructed in that time frame. The coal was examined by coal dealers and manufacturers in Chattanooga before it was transported by rail to Coalburn, Alabama, where it could be made into coke.

With the discovery of vast deposits of bituminous coal, Durham eventually evolved into Durham Coal and Coke Company, a town with the company providing housing, company store, and company-built churches. By 1910 Durham had a butcher shop, a movie theatre, gambling hall, pool hall, barber shop, ice house and three boarding houses for the miners. Business was so brisk that newcomers had to wait six months for a company house to become vacant. The Durham post office was listed as Pittsburgh, Georgia, and was in operation from 1900 until 1946.

After the first coal shipment was made in 1892, the mining of coal continued on and off until the 1940s. The Chickamauga Coke Ovens are still present today just north of downtown Chickamauga on Georgia Highway 341. Twice a day trips were made hauling coal by the trains to the ovens where it would be burned at high temperatures without any oxygen present to remove the impurities from the coal.

In order to make iron and steel, coke is necessary because it burns longer, hotter and steadier that coal. This was what the foundries needed in the Chattanooga market. By 1904 the Durham mines were producing 700 to 1000 tons of coke in the Chickamauga ovens every day with approximately 1/5 of the ore being manufactured into coke. This process continued operations into the Great Depression years when the large seam of coal eventually ran out.

The railroad was abandoned in 1951. The narrow iron rails on the Chickamauga and Durham line were taken up, and the wooden trestles rotted. During the coal boom of the 1970s, in the ugly practice of strip mining, coal was extracted from the area.

While the rails were removed in 1952, a majority of the former right-of-way can still be traced, although some of it has been encroached on and part of it goes through a private nature preserve. Eventually the right of way was given to Walker County. Plans to build a walking trail from Chickamauga to Lula Falls were originally withdrawn because of opposition from land owners along the property.

A one-day trip to visit the Town of Chickamauga and the coke ovens can be an interesting and historical journey.

EROSION OF MCLEMORE COVE

On top of and below the intersection of Pigeon Mountain and Lookout Mountain lies the picturesque valley of McLemore Cove in Walker County, Georgia.

Before it was divided into individual tracts after being part of the multi-billion dollar estate of the Orkin Pest Control empire of O. Wayne Rollins, it possessed many of the natural characteristics of the better known Cades Cove area in the Great Smokey Mountain National Park in Tennessee.

The history of McLemore Cove goes back to its Native American Indian and European settlers. The cove was named for two brothers, Robert and John McLemore, who were sons of a white trader and a Cherokee Indian mother. John McLemore was a Cherokee Chief and Captain of the United States Army.

The land was originally purchased by the State of Georgia through treaties with the Cherokee Nation. From 1805 to 1832, Georgia lotteries were held and tracts of land of 160 acres were sold to settlers and homesteaders.

The virgin beauty of the Cove resulted in approximately 3,440 acres being purchased by an Athens Georgia attorney who owned 31 slaves and built and maintained a Southern mansion until it was foreclosed in 1899.

The Civil War resulted in another major mistake by the Confederacy which involved McLemore Cove and which might have altered or delayed the final conclusion of the nationwide conflict.

On September 10 and 11, 1963, Union General William Rosecrans' army was comprised of three corps under Generals Thomas Crittenden, George Thomas and Alexander Cook. The three groups were located respectively in Chattanooga, Stephens Gap on Lookout Mountain and the town of Alpine, Georgia. An attack on one of them by Confederate troops could have resulted in a disaster that might have altered the outcome of the conflict in the South. Rosecrans fell for a trap set by Confederate General Braxton Bragg and sent General Thomas' corps into McLemore Cove, which was a canyon like area created by the junction of Lookout and Pigeon Mountains.

Due to a mix-up in orders by southern generals Hindman and Hill, the Union troops were able to escape and the Battle of Chickamauga occurred on September 19-20, 1863, without the loss of 1-2 divisions of the 12 which comprised Rosecrans army. Although considered a Confederate victory, if it had been fully successful, the Chickamauga conflict might have delayed the defeat of the South at Chattanooga and Missionary Ridge and further delayed the Union advance to Atlanta.

After the Civil War, the farm was sold several times for various reasons such as farming, harvesting of timber and raising prized cattle. Around 1968, Orkin Exterminating billionaire O. Wayne Rollins, Ringgold, Georgia native, accumulated a tract of at least 11,500 acres of the bottom land and surrounding mountain area adjoining the Crockford-Pigeon Mountain Wildlife Management Area. The management area is owned by the State of Georgia and comprises 20,657 acres of Lookout Mountain acreage.

Rollins restored the original mansion, built a landing strip to expedite his trips from Atlanta, raised prize Hereford cattle and maintained the beautiful natural setting of the Cove in its picturesque condition until his death in 1991. A family battle over the disposition of the eight billion dollar estate created by Wayne Rollins commenced shortly after his death. It resulted in the sale of the Rollins property to two Summerville land developers who sub-divided the property into mini-farms of various sizes and for the erection of fine country homes.

In 2008, Walker County purchased approximately 280 acres of a 1,800 acre acquisition for $10.5 million dollars jointly owned by the county, state and preservation trusts.

The legal battles arising out of the failure of Hutcheson Medical Center and the financial problems of Walker County continue to this day as the residents of the entire county absorb the financial woes of the unsuccessful development of the Rollins property and increased property taxes.

In 2005, a book entitled *Echoes of McLemore Cove,* written by local historian and Cove resident Vera Frances Cannon Coulter with the support of the Walker County Historic Preservation Commission and published by Waldenhouse Publishers, Inc., depicts an effort to preserve for posterity the history and heritage of this unique area of Walker County, which comprised the McLemore Cove Historic District. The district is listed on the National Register of Historic Places and consists of a 50,141 acre community with 293 contributing historic sites.

Unfortunately, its development has greatly reduced the area's favorable comparison to the Cades Cove area owned by the federal government in the Smokies.

WALKER COUNTY COURTHOUSE WAR

Time has erased the events that occurred in Chattanooga's neighboring county in Northwest Georgia about the judicial and political war over the building of a new and present courthouse.

Beginning in 1883, Walker County was run by a five-member commission serving two-year terms. In 1916 the terms were changed to four years, and in 1940, showing the flexibility of the electorate to form new governments, all authority was placed in the hands of one commissioner. In 2018 Walker County voters approved a referendum to transition from a sole commissioner who had both legislative and executive powers to a four-member board of commissioners elected by district. The first members of the board were elected in November 2020 and took office in January 2021.

A Walker County grand jury on March 26, 1915, unfavorably reported on conditions at the old courthouse and recommended the erection of a new courthouse to Judge Moses Wright. As a result of the grand jury recommendation, the Walker County Board of Commissioners voted to erect a new courthouse, and the voters of the county approved a bond drive to fund the cost of building the structure.

This is where the real controversy begins. Not everyone agreed where the new courthouse would be located. Those opposed to Lafayette were mostly from the northern end of the county and wanted the county seat moved to Chickamauga or at least closer to Rossville and Chattanooga. Interesting legal proceedings followed. A representative of Chickamauga filed a petition against the commissioners and numerous businesses that were involved with the courthouse bid in an effort to stop the project.

Judge Moses Wright of the Rome Circuit Court had jurisdiction of the case, but the opponents of the project did some creative "judge shopping" and hired the judge's brother, Robert Wright of Chattanooga, as their attorney. This was an attempt to create a conflict of interest that would disqualify Judge Moses Wright from the case, since they knew that he favored the courthouse construction bill. Judge Wright denied the petition to recuse himself from the case, and the Georgia Supreme Court affirmed him.

In another surprise move, the anti-courthouse supporters took their petition to Judge A.W. Fite in the Cherokee Circuit Court and asked him to remove Judge Wright from the case. Fite agreed and issued an order to that effect, took over the case, and issued a temporary restraining order against the commissioners, stopping any further work on the courthouse project.

On May 26, 1916, the litigation got further heated when Judge Fite issued a contempt of court ruling against the Board of Commissioners and the publisher of the *Walker County Messenger*, E.P. Hall, Jr., who had published a request for bids for work to be performed on the courthouse project.

Judge Wright immediately intervened in the case asserting that his court was the proper one to try the litigation and issued an injunction against the anti-courthouse group. He also banned any Georgia sheriff or their deputies from acting on any orders from Judge Fite.

Undeterred by Judge Fite's ruling, the Board of Commissioners contacted a construction company from Anniston, Alabama, to begin the project – "at once." This resulted in a large crowd of citizens assembling on June 6, 1916, for the awarding of the builder's contract. Also present was Sheriff Ward of Catoosa County who had been ordered by Judge Fite to arrest O.M. Clemmons, clerk of the Superior Court if he should issue any process initiating the start of work on the courthouse project.

When Clemmons refused to go voluntarily with the sheriff to Ringgold, Sheriff Ward and his support group of opposition constituents left town. From this point the legal (or illegal) proceedings really heated up on the question of which judge had jurisdiction over Walker County's new courthouse.

Sheriff Ward returned from Catoosa County and roped off the construction project area. Commissioner J.D. McConnell was confronted with a shotgun when he arrived at the scene and was arrested when he refused to voluntarily go to Ringgold to address Judge Fite's contempt of court citation. That night, Sheriff Ward and his two deputies arrested two of the commissioners, S.P. Hall and John M. Ransom, and took them to Ringgold.

As a counter action Walker County, Sheriff R.S. Garmany went to Chickamauga on Judge Wright's orders, overruling Judge Fite's orders, and arrested S.T. Carson. He then unsuccessfully tried to arrest J.S. Alsobrook in Rossville, but he had fled to Tennessee where he could not be arrested.

On June 30, 1916, Judge Fite, before a large crowd, tried the three commissioners in Ringgold in contempt of court charges. Sensing the seriousness of the situation, he set bonds of $1,000 in each case and would release them from paying that amount if they would revoke the courthouse contract. The three refused, and Judge Fite ordered them jailed.

Judge Fite then conveniently left the proceedings under the pretense of a "speaking engagement" and passed the hot potato to the Catoosa County Sheriff to put the three in custody. The Catoosa County Sheriff refused, and the commissioners returned to Lafayette. In the meantime, Judge Wright issued an order to the Walker County Sheriff to "Provide ample means for fully protecting members of the County Board as well as the contractors working on the new courthouse and to jail for contempt anyone interfering with the courthouse project."

The Georgia Supreme Court entered the fray and in two orders resolved the judicial war between Judge Wright and Judge Fite. On December 22, 1916, the High Court reversed Judge Fite's restraining order on building the new courthouse, and on April 2, 1917, the Court held that Judge Fite had no jurisdiction over the case. This reaffirmed its previous ruling that Judge Wright was not disqualified, and Judge Fite's order adjudging the Walker Court commissioners in contempt was invalid, and it was dismissed.

Strangely one of Sheriff Ward's deputies was held in contempt of Judge Wright's order in helping the Sheriff the make the arrest. Because the Georgia Supreme Court also held that the Sheriff of Catoosa County had no legal authority to serve arrest papers in Walker County, Sheriff Ward escaped prosecution.

On April 23, 1918, the new Walker County Courthouse was formally dedicated after construction costs of $80,000. It was lauded as "the most magnificent edifice in the county."

Judge Moses Wright made a formal speech at the dedication before a large crowd. Judge A.W. Fite was conspicuously absent.

Seems like things do not change much in the Lookout Judicial Circuit!

DAISY'S TIES TO LAST GEORGIA LEGAL HANGING

The last legal hanging in the State of Georgia that took place in Lafayette on April 27, 1923, has close ties to the north Hamilton County town of Daisy and ultimately the twin cities of Soddy Daisy.

On March 19, 1922, Walker County Deputy Sheriff Joseph W. Morton was killed at the Durham railroad depot as he waited for his daughter Mary Ann to bring his young granddaughter Christen to him on the train. The child had injured her right hand, and they planned to take her to the local doctor for treatment.

George Baker (22) and his younger brother, Ralph (15) were two moonshiners who had lost their hidden still in a mountain cave where it was discovered and destroyed by Morton. One story was that the Bakers were on the incoming train to rob it, and that when it arrived at the Durham station, they confronted Morton about whether he had an arrest warrant for them. An altercation and a shootout resulted in the deputy's death.

Conflicting stories exist as to who fired the fatal shots at Deputy Morton. The boys fled and later were apprehended separately. They were almost killed by an angry lynch mob. However Sheriff Harmon was able to transport them to Rome for safekeeping.

On April 20, 1922, two trials that took only three hours from jury selection to verdict were held in the courthouse in Lafayette. Ralph Baker testified in George's case that he shot Deputy Morton in defense of George after the law officer shot at his brother. George did not testify, and the defense lawyers put on limited proof.

One important witness that could have possibly helped substantiate that Ralph shot Morton in self-defense of his brother was never called or revealed to the defense by law enforcement officers who were told of his existence and testimony. In today's justice system, such non-disclosure would be sufficient to get the Bakers a new trial.

Within one hour of deliberations, the Walker County jury found both boys guilty of first degree murder, and they were sentenced to hang. Appeals to the Georgia Supreme Court were denied, and preparations were made for their executions.

A reporter for the *New York Times* started a nationwide crusade on behalf of the boys on the grounds that George was of "unsound mentality both by reason of nerve trouble brought on by meningitis and by inheritance." He also claimed that Ralph, being only 15 years of age, was too young to be put to death.

On April 10, 1923, a clemency hearing was held before Georgia Governor T.W. Hardwick, and on April 27 he commuted Ralph's sentence to life imprisonment but affirmed George's death sentence.

On April 27, 1923, George was hung at the Walker County jail and taken to Wann's Chapel Funeral Home where his body was viewed by mourners and curious spectators in crowds estimated to be between 600-1,000 attendees. Prior to his death, George claimed to be innocent but urged the youth present, "Stay away from liquor and bad associates."

The Chattanooga Times reported that more than 1,500 cars jammed the roads from the funeral home to the rural Morris Hills Baptist Church Cemetery in East Brainerd where George was laid to rest.

Ralph Baker was released from prison around 1935-1936. He always maintained that he was the one who shot Deputy Morton in defense of his brother.

Morton descendant, Marnie L. Pehrson, in 2009 wrote *An Uncertain Justice* about the case and discussed the trial. She also revealed a connection to the Soddy Daisy area. Her great grandparents were Sherman Morton (grandson of Deputy Morton) and Edna Jane Springfield Morton. The book is still available on Amazon.

Sherman would become an engineer on the Southern Railroad and a successful land developer in the Daisy area. He was also credited with helping many residents obtain jobs with the railroad. When the cities of Soddy and Daisy became a municipality in 1969, Morton served as one of the original commissioners and was active until his death on April 12, 1996, at the age of 91. His wife Edna has preceded him in death in 1975.

The disputed facts have contributed to the historical lore of the last legal hanging in the State of Georgia.

BEATEN BY A BITE – GENE TALMADGE

Prior to the United Supreme Court decision in Baker v. Carr 369 U.S.186 (1962,) which loosened the stronghold that rural communities held over the urban large cities, one of the most powerful politicians in Georgia would be Eugene Talmadge.

Talmadge was born in 1884 in Forsyth, Georgia. He came from an upper class family, but he always claimed to be the champion of the lower class rural white citizens. He actively promoted segregation and white supremacy and was an avid opponent of President Franklin Delano Roosevelt's New Deal as a Southern conservative Democrat.

He and his successor, Marvin Griffin, were the darlings of the "wool hat boys" who primarily consisted of southern white men who after the Civil War had returned home to find that after the freeing of their slaves they had to do their own plowing, hoeing and picking.

The Confederate veterans stubbornly refused to wear the cool, wide-brim straw field hats favored by the former slaves. Instead the white farmers wore sweaty, narrow-brim wool hats, so that the boiling Southern sun would turn their "necks red" when they bent over to work.

Gene Talmadge was a master at playing to the poor, rural voters. In spite of his family wealth, he would arrive for courthouse rallies in worn-out cars, pushed by a gang of supporters because he didn't have enough money to buy gas to get into town. He always wore a rumpled suit, and his black hair would be lying lank across his forehead in an unruly fashion.

Gene on the speaking platform would point his fist, stirring up the crowd with his anti-city and segregation rhetoric. He would close by taking off his coat and revealing his trademark, a pair of flame red galluses holding up his britches. He cultivated the image of "the wild man from Sugar Creek."

On one occasion his boasting about being a country man possibly cost him an election.

Talmadge, for some reason, liked to boast about having to answer a call from Mother Nature by relieving himself in the woods. On the way to give an important campaign speech in Moultrie, Georgia, Gene told his driver to stop the car so he could relieve himself in the bushes. While he was performing the necessary act, a black widow spider bit him on his privates and almost killed him.

Gene became so weak that he couldn't give his usual fiery speech and had to let someone else give his speech. He later would claim that it cost him the governorship. Ellis Arnall won the race, and Gene, like any politician, had an explanation for his loss.

In a post-election interview with his political nemesis, *Atlanta Constitution* Editor Ralph McGill (of Soddy), he said that Arnall would not have beaten him, "If that black widow spider hadn't bitten me on the b_ _ _ _."

Are modern day Georgia politics as interesting?

LULA LAKE MURDERS – 1963

On the Georgia side of Lookout Mountain lies the very picturesque and beautiful rural property that is now owned by the Lula Lake Land Trust. The trust was formed in 1994 primarily through the efforts of Robert (Bobby) Davenport, a member of the second generation of the family that founded the Krystal Company, a fast food restaurant chain in the South.

Originally, the initial tract of land purchase was over 1,000 acres. Its size has now increased to over 8,000 acres. Through the efforts of Bobby Davenport, what was once a dumping ground for garbage, burned out stolen automobiles, and a popular lovers lane is now a scenic natural site that is available to the public under the supervision and control of the Land Trust created by him prior to his unexpected death in 1994.

The waters of Rock Creek Gorge tumble downward into Lula Lake, and when the water is sufficient, it tumbles over Lula Falls on its descent to the Lookout Valley below. Open to the public on a limited basis, there is no charge for admission, but charitable donations are welcomed. This rustic site was also the venue for one of the most highly publicized murder cases in the history of the region.

A young couple, Orville (Pete) Steele, age 19, and his girlfriend, Carolyn Newell, age 16, on Sunday, April 14, 1963, had gone to Lula Lake. Their bodies were found six days later after a massive search in the community had taken place.

Pete Steele's body was tied to a tree and he died of strangulation with the use of twine and a wooden stick tightened around his neck. Some 100-150 feet from Pete's body lay the remains of Carolyn Newell with her wrists bound together with twine. She had been raped several times, struck in the head and then choked to death. The grisly scene revealed that she was naked from the waist down, and wild animals had eaten part of her leg.

Suspicion immediately directed towards twenty-seven year old James Blevins, who later admitted he would drive to Lookout Mountain and spy on young couples who engaged in sexual intercourse. He was picked up for questioning and admitted that he had talked to the couple, but he denied any involvement in their murders.

He was charged with two counts of First Degree Murder, held without bond and was housed in the jail at Rome, Georgia, because of rumored threats against him in Walker County. The State of Georgia elected to try the Carolyn Newell case first, and the Pete Steele case was put on hold until the Newell case was concluded. Thus the stage was set for a prosecutorial mistake that would ultimately result in Blevins being acquitted of both murders.

The case was prosecuted on behalf of the State of Georgia by attorney general, Earl Self, and special prosecutor from Summerville, the legendary Bobby Lee Cook. James Blevins was defended by another great of the Georgia Bar, Colonel Frank Gleason of Rossville, who was an aggressive and tenacious trial lawyer. A case that attracted not only local and state media coverage, it also was picked up by the *New York Times*.

In a hotly contested trial by outstanding lawyers, Blevins was found guilty of the Newell murder and sentenced to death by electrocution. On appeal, the conviction was overturned on the ground that "The selection of jurors must be drawn in open court." By analogy, a new trial was granted because "The indictment charging Blevins with murder was likewise not returned in open court but was handed to the court clerk in the trial judge's office."

A second trial was held in the case, and Blevins was acquitted. The State of Georgia next attempted to try the defendant in the Pete Steele case, but the prosecution made the mistake of not giving Blevins a trial "within two regular terms of court after the term for which he had filed a demand for trial" as required by Georgia statute.

In a decision based on a technicality, the Georgia Court of Appeals on March 11, 1966, held that Blevins' "right to a speedy trial" had been denied and that the murder charge in the Pete Steele case had to be dismissed, thus freeing James Blevins.

Pulitzer Prize winning writer, Cormac McCarthy, is alleged to have repeatedly relied on the facts of the Blevins murder case when he wrote his novel *Child of God* which closely parallels the historical details in the actual murder in northwest Georgia at the site which is now the Lula Lake Land Trust.

Since the location is now generally closed to the public after dark, little facts are known as to whether the ghosts of Carolyn Newell and Pete Steele are present on the beautiful and tranquil premises.

Beautiful Lula Lake Falls on Lookout Mountain, Georgia

Conclusion

The 76 articles contained in the book are just a small sampling of the rich histories of the states of Tennessee, Alabama, and Georgia.

As I researched the stories contained, I was often led to another one contained within the original article.

Hopefully, the reader will continue to explore and discover other unique events and interesting individuals in the Tri-States.

History Sources in Our Area

I am taking the risk of not mentioning some of the outstanding authors of articles and books that will inform readers and newcomers to the history of the Tennessee, Alabama, and Georgia areas. Any oversight is not intentional.

Any history of Hamilton County, Tennessee must begin with Dr. James W. Livingood's, 1981 book *A History of Hamilton County, Tennessee* (Memphis State University Press).

The *Chattanooga Regional Historical Journal* in another excellent publication that comes with a yearly membership to the Chattanooga Area Historical Association that can be obtained with a $20.00 individual membership and purchase of copies of old and new journals for $5.00 and $6.00. Many of the best historians regularly send in articles and include, Sam Elliott, Harmon Jolley, Gay Morgan Moore, Kay Baker Gaston, Roy Morris, Jr., David Moon, Dean W. Arnold, LaVonne Jolley, Chuck Hamilton, Smith Murray, Maury Nicely, Mickey Robbins, Anthony Hodges, Mark Kennedy, Billy Parker, David Carroll, and Alex McKeel, to just name a few.

The surrounding counties in Tennessee, Alabama and Georgia have societies that contain much of the history in their area and several have museums that display many items pertaining to local events.

The Chattanooga Public Library under the leadership of Corrine Hill has a wealth of history information including back copies of former and existing newspapers. The staff is always helpful, and Suzette Raney is a regular article contributor.

Linda Moss Mines is the current Hamilton County Historian and is a weekly contributor of an article in the "Perspective" Section each Sunday in the *Chattanooga Times/Free Press*. Mark Kennedy is also a member of the local paper that writes timely historical articles.

John Shearer and the author contribute historical articles under the "Happenings" Section in the *Chattanoogan.com* web paper of John Wilson. Roy Exum, when not writing about politics, will also contribute a historical article.

John Wilson is likewise a former Hamilton County Historian and his published works, *Chattanooga's Story* (1980); *Scenic Historic Lookout Mountain* (1977); *Railroads in and Around Chattanooga* (2017); *The Remarkable Stokes Collection* (2014); *Hamilton County Pioneers* (2017) and *Early Hamilton Settlers* (2018) all contain photos and important historical data.

The Paul Heiner's *Historic Chattanooga* (2016) contains over 3000 photos of Chattanooga and can be seen on the Chattanooga Public Library website.

Spokesman David Moon's *Picnooga.com* contains 16,000 current and 13,000 potential digitized photos that were donated to the Public Library or Chattanooga History Center when the *Chattanooga Times* and *Chattanooga News Free Press* were merged in 1999. They are available for viewing on the website.

Sam Hall in 2014 created a website that is now known as *Chattanooga History.com* that is another source of additional information on the history of our area.

David Carroll and Earl Freudenberg often make valuable contributions about the history of the media in our hometown.

If you want to check on history on a statewide basis a $35.00 membership with the Tennessee Historical Society will get you a copy of the *Tennessee Historical Quarterly*.

The specific information on how to contact each of the sources mentioned in this article can be found by going to Google Chrome and inserting the name of the individuals in the publication in Chattanooga, Tennessee.

By logging in on any of the above you will enter a world of knowledge and history about the present topics, persons, and events in the State of Tennessee we proudly call home as well as in the states of Alabama and Georgia.

Enjoy your trip.

The Author

Jerry H. Summers is a practicing attorney in Chattanooga, Tennessee. He has served as an assistant district attorney and municipal judge since he began the practice of law in 1966. His entire life has been lived in Chattanooga, Tennessee except for seven years in St. Petersburg, Florida, between the ages of seven and fourteen.

He has argued cases before the United States and Tennessee Supreme courts and has been involved in numerous landmark decisions in both civil and criminal law.

His peers in the legal profession have elected him to membership in the International Academy of Trial Lawyers, American College of Trial Lawyers, International Society of Barristers, American Board of Trial Advocates, American Board of Criminal Lawyers, and he has been selected every year since 1981 as one of the Best Lawyers in America for the 40th consecutive year in both personal injury and criminal law. In 2019 he was selected as a Fellow in the American Academy of Appellate Lawyers. In 2021, he was chosen to receive the Lifetime Achievement Award by the Tennessee Trial Lawyers Association.

By an unsolicited vote of the lawyers of Tennessee, he has consistently been selected as one of the "Best 100 Lawyers in Tennessee" and "Mid-South Super Lawyers."

Orange Grove Center and the Chattanooga Bar Association have both honored him as Philanthropist of the Year for his community work. In 2007 he was selected as Distinguished Alumnus at the Centennial Celebration of Chattanooga Central High School, and in 2021 he was inducted into Central's Sports Hall of Fame.

In 2014 he was honored by being designated as the Distinguished Alumnus at the University of the South at Sewanee, and in 2016 the University of Tennessee at Knoxville designated him as one of the Distinguished Alumnus at that institution.

*Tri-State Trivia Reflection*s is his seventh published book and discusses historical persons, places and events in Tennessee, Alabama, and Georgia. His first literary effort released in 2014 titled *The Turtle and the Lawyer* was an attempt to thank those individuals and entities that have helped him in life and to suggest respectfully that the reader do the same.

His second and third publications were biographies of the controversial Judge Raulston Schoolfield titled *Rush to Justice? Tennessee's Forgotten Trial of the Century – Schoolfield 1958* and *Schoolfield: Out of the Ashes 1958-1982*. A tribute to Central football Coach Stanley J. Farmer titled *We Called Him Coach* was his fourth book. The story of the 1958 Chattanooga Central basketball team that lost the 1958 Tennessee State Championship game by one point entitled *One Shot Short* is his fifth book. The 2020 compilation of short historical articles titled *Tennessee Trivia No. 1* is his sixth.

In 2021 he was selected for the James W. Livingood Historian of the Year Award by the Chattanooga Area Historical Association.

Book number eight, *Prepare to Win – Get Ready to Appeal*, under review by the University of Tennessee College of Law, has been accepted for publication. It will be a compilation of appellate decisions that have changed Tennessee law from the City Court of Chattanooga to the Tennessee and United States Supreme Courts. Four of those cases have been decided favorably by the U.S. Supreme Court (2 civil and 2 criminal) beginning in 1972. The purpose of this book is to motivate attorneys to raise novel constitutional issues for possible appellate review.

Orange Grove Center, its staff and its clients are some of those that have had a profound effect on Summers' life.

Index

A

Albert, Eddie 168
Alexander, Governor Lamar 91
Allen, Jack 205
Alpine, Georgia 224
Alsobrook, J.S. 229
Anderson, Robert Charles "Doc" 167
Arnall, Ellis 235
Arnold, Dean W. 239
Austin, Ruby Lee Folsom Ellis 139

B

Babe Ruth 24
Baker, E. B. 173
Baker, George 231
Baker, John 32
Baker, "Preach" 214
Baker, Ralph 231
Bancroft, Anne 122
Barbour County 141
Barker, Jess 195
Barnes, Margaret Anne 146
Barrett, Cleve 214
Bates, Ruby 150
Battle of Ringgold Gap 170, 217
Bean, Crawford 43, 44
Bee Tree Shoals 112
Bell, "Cool" Papa 71
Bell, Dr. Alexander Graham 123
Bessemer, Alabama 129
Bevis, "Red" 213
Billings, C. L. 214
Birmingham, Alabama 23, 103, 104, 114, 115, 132, 135, 137, 142, 178
Black Draught Laxative Product 60
Blairsville, Georgia 203, 205, 206
Blevins, James 237
Booth, Shirley 194
Boyd, Helen 171

Boys, Scottsboro 150
Boys, Wool Hat 192, 193, 234, 250
Bradshaw, Thelma Finster 178
Bragg, General Braxton 170, 225
Braswell, Mary 62
Bridgeport, Alabama, 99, 108
Bridges, Dr. R. R. 162
Bright, Fletcher 32
Brodsky, Joseph 161
Brown, Thomas Marion 75
Brown v. City of Chattanooga 53
Brushy Mountain 77, 91, 92, 93, 243
Bryant, Paul "Bear" 126
Buckle of the Bible Belt 53, 60
Buff, Ricky 211
Burch, "Lonesome" 214
Burton, Thomas 66
Byrd, Councilman Anthony 90

C

Caldwell, Dr. J. Frank 97
Calise, Sarah 90
Callahan, Judge William 152
Canton, Georgia 160
Carmichael, A. A. 156
Carroll, David 239
Carrolton, Georgia 194, 195
Carson, Johnny 177
Carson, S.T. 229
Carter, Dan 158
Carver, George Washington 186
Case, Samuel 214
Cash, Johnny 15, 35, 51, 84, 189, 190, 191
Cash, June Carter 15, 189
Chalkey, Eaton 195
Chamblee, George W. 158
Chambliss, Alexander W. 158

Chaplin, Charlie 180
Chapman, Janice 164
Chase, Hal 25
Chattanooga Area Historical Association 239
Chattanooga Medicine Company 59, 60, 61, 244
Chattanoogan.com 12
Cherokee 102, 105, 109, 116, 217, 218, 219, 222, 224, 228, 244
Chickamauga Dam 111
Chickamauga Island 111
Chilton, Dr. Ken 90
Cicotte, Eddie 25
Clarke County 207, 208
Clark, Major William H. 218
Clark, Paul 16
Clark, Tom 25
Cleburne, General Patrick 170, 217
Clemens, John and Jane Lampton 29
Clemens, Samuel L. 29
Clement, Governor Frank G. 64
Clemmons, O.M. 228
Cloudmont 98
coal mines 91, 244
Coca-Cola 176
cockfighting 45, 49, 244
Colbert County. 122
Colbert Shoals Canal Lock 112
Cole, Lynette 76
Coleman, Warren 214
Cole, Randall 164
Columbia, Tennessee 75
Columbus, Georgia 144, 182
Conley, Jim 197
Coogan, Steve 180
Cook, Alexander 224
Cook, Bobby Lee 200
Coon Dog Cemetery 116
coonhound 116, 118, 244
Coppinger, Ty 214
Cotton Ball 194

Coulter, Vera Frances Cannon 226
Crittenden, Generals Thomas 224
Crockford-Pigeon Mountain Wildlife Management Area 225
Cruise, Tom 92
Crump, E.H. (Boss) 21
Cullman, Alabama 136

D

Dade County 172, 173
Dade, Independent State of 172
Daisy 67, 214, 231, 232, 244, 249
Dallas Island 111
Darrow, Clarence 160
Davenport, Robert (Bobby) 236
Davis, Congressman John 186
Davis, Edward E. 39
Davis, Jimmy 170
Day, Doris 168
Dean, Carl 170
Decatur, Alabama, 149, 152
de Graffenried, Ryan 148
de Havilland, Olivia 194
DeKalb, Baron 102
Dekalb County 98, 244
Denton, Buford "Lefty" 213
Depot Days 100
DeSoto Falls 98, 104, 244
Dickerson, Bob 32
Dolly Parton 95, 170
Dolly Pond Church of God 66
Dorian, Major James 108
Doty, Duncan 214
Douglas, Phil Brooks 23, 24, 26
Dragging Canoe 78
Drano Murder 164, 166, 244
Duke, Patty 122
Duncan, Harold 45
Durham 222, 223, 231, 244
Dyer, Herschel A. 204
Dyer, M. C. 204

Dyer, Micajah Clark 203, 205, 206, 207
Dyer, Morena Ownbey 204

E

Eddy, Nelson 140
Edmiston, Parker 101
Edward, Bobby 190
Eiselstein, Bill 34
Eisenhower, Dwight D. 145, 168
Elba, Alabama 140
Ellington, Governor Buford 21
Elliott, Sam 239
Ellis, Jim 211
Ellison's Cave 220
Ellis, Paul 214
End of the Line 93
Engel, Joe 214
Enterprise, Alabama 140
Epps, Ben 207, 208, 209
Etter, E.B. "Red" 137
Evans, H. Clay 59
Exum, Roy 240

F

Falwell, Jerry 187
Fantastic Pit 220, 221, 245
Farmer, Stanley J. 137
Finster, Howard 175, 177, 178
Finster, Lula Alice Henegar 175
Finster, William 175
Fite, A.W. 228
flying machine 203, 207, 245
Flynt, Larry 38
Folsom, Cornelia Ellis Snevely 136
Folsom, James Elisha "Big Jim" 135, 136
Folsom, "Big" Ruby 136, 139
Folsom, Sarah Carnley 135
Ford, Henry 176
Ford, Lewis Francis 66
Forrest, General Nathan Bedford 172
Forsyth, Georgia 234

Fort Benning 144
Fort Harker 99, 245
Fort Payne 102, 103, 104, 164, 165, 166, 245, 248
Fowler, Cecil 214
Frank, Leo 197, 197, 198, 199
Franklin Delano Roosevelt 111, 234
Freedom Riders 147
Freeman, Pauline 175
French, Robert B. 165
Freudenberg, Earl 240
Fricke, Janie 16
Fuller, Albert 145
Fulmer, Phil 76

G

Gabor, Eva 168
Galbreath, Charles "Charlie" 37
Garland, Edward (Eddie) T. M. 201, 202
Garland, John A. 202
Garland, Reuben A. (Rube) 200, 201
Garmany, R.S. 229
Garrett, Archer Ferrell 145
Garrett, Silas 145
Gaston, Kay Baker 239
Gibson, Josh 71
Gleason, Colonel Frank 237
Glenwood Manor 5, 72
Goethals, George Washington 112
Goodman, James 158
Grady, Allan 146
Graham, Barbara 194
Grant, Tillman 39
Grasshopper, Tennessee 66
Graves, Congressman Tom 185
Graves, Governor Bibb 156
Green, Dr. Thomas Fitzgerald 204
Greene, Marjorie Taylor 185
Greensboro, Alabama 155
Griffin, Marvin 192, 234

Grisham, John 92
Grosvenor, Gilbert H. 109
Guild 27, 77, 83, 245
Guild, Joseph Conn 77

H

Hales Bar 77, 78, 79, 83, 84, 246
Haletown, Tennessee 51, 77, 83
Hall, E.P. 228
Hall, Sam 240
Hall, S.P. 229
Hamblin, Pastor Andrew 67
Hamilton, Chuck 239
Hamilton County 39, 42, 66, 67, 72, 80, 88, 111, 112, 159, 160, 173, 231, 239, 240
Hammond, Ben 98
Hancock, John 164
Hardwick, Governor T.W. 232
Hardy, Oliver Norvell 179
Harlem, Georgia 179
Harold Duncan 45, 46
Harris, Bernie 39
Harvey, Bob 170
Hawkins, A. E. 159
Hawkins, E. A. 152
Haydock, Adam 221
Hayes, Joy 12
Hayward, Susan 194
Halem, Georgia 179
Head, Sheriff Grady 66
Heflin, Howell 132, 148
Heflin, James Thomas 132
Heflin, Robert Stell 132
Heiner, Paul 240
Heisman, John 119, 121
Helms, Senator Jessie 187
Henderson, Katie 215
Hendricks, George G. "Buddy" 42
Hess, Rudolph 187
Heston, Charlton 168

Hiatt, John 92
High Museum of Art 178
Hill, Corrine 240
Hinckley, John 133
Hodges, Anthony 239
Hollins, Senator Fritz 133
Hooker, General Joseph 217
Hoover, Herbert 208
Hoover, J. Edgar 145
Hopkins, Anthony 92
Horton, James Edwin, Jr. 149
Hotel Tutwiler 114, 115, 135, 246, 250
Howard, Gene 148
Hunt, Nelson Bunker 187
Hustler Magazine 38, 39, 40, 246
Hutcheson, John L. 210
Hutton, Timothy 162

I

Independent State of Dade 172
Ives, Burl 168
Ivey, Governor Kay 165

J

Jackson, Shoeless Joe 25
James, Fob 136, 165
Jarnaigan, Lester "Son" 213
Jefferson, Arthur Stanley 179
Jemison, Robert 114
Jennings, Waylon 15
jitney cabs 56, 57, 246
Johnson, Christine 135
Johnson, Walter "Big Train" 23
Jolley, Harmon 80, 239
Jolley, LaVonne 239
Jones, George 170
Jones, James Earl 70
Jones, Sheriff Ralph 189, 191
Jordanaires 16
Jordan, Ralph "Shug" 127
Joyce, Arnold, "Sammy"

K

Keller, Helen Adams 122, 123, 124, 125, 203, 204, 205, 207, 245
Kennedy, John F. 147
Kennedy, Mark 239, 240
Killian, Bill 50
Killian, Herman Brown "Yap" 48
Killian, Mike 50
Knight, Thomas E. 150, 155
Koger, Eddie 213
Kristofferson, Chris 15
Kury, 1st Lt. Jake 215

L

Ladds, Tennessee 83, 247
Lafayette, Georgia 231
Lance, James Washington 204
Landis, Kennesaw Mountain 24
Laurel and Hardy 179
Laurel, Stan 179
Lauter, Walt 210, 214
Lebowitz, Samuel 153
Lector, Dr. Hannibal 92
Lee, Newt 197
Lee, Robert E. 172
Lincoln Park 71, 88, 89, 90, 247
Lindbergh, Charles 114
Little River Canyon 104
Lively, J.J. 159
Livingood, Dr. James W. 239
Lombardi, Vince 127
Long, Elizabeth 80
Looper, Byron "Low Tax" 91
Lula Lake 236, 238, 247
Lynch, Dr. Marvin 162

M

Maddow, V.W. "Red" 42
Magill, R.C. 217
Magnani, Anna 194
Makris, Patricia Short 87
Man in Black 15, 189, 191, 247
Mantle, Mickey 32, 33
Marion County 48, 49, 50, 51, 77, 79, 110
Marrenner, Edythe 194
Mason, John 97
Mathis, Larry 95
May, Brian 91
Mays, Willie 70
McAllister, Henry Hill 21
McCampbell, David 129, 130
McCarthy, Cormac 238
McCarthy, Senator Joe "Tailgunner" 186
McConnell, J.D. 228
McCoy, Bob 210
McDonald, Larry Patton 185
McDonald, Frank 32
McGill, Ralph 235
McGowan, Ben 12
McGraw, John 24
McKeel, Alex 239
McLemore Cove 224, 225, 226, 247
McLemore, John 224
McLemore, Robert 224
McReynolds, Howard 48
Mears, "Stormy" 49
Medal of Honor 129, 130, 131, 182, 183, 247
Mentone, Alabama 97, 98, 247
Milledgeville, Georgia. 179
Millers ball team 213, 214, 247, 248
Millican, Lisa 164
Millsaps, Willard 214
Mines, Linda Moss 240
Mitchell, Mayor R. A. 106
Monroe, Marilyn 176
Montague, Theodore G. 59
Montgomery, Alabama 150, 156
Moody, Milo 159
Moon, David 239, 240

moonshine 42, 43, 54, 93, 94, 247
Moore, Gay Morgan 239
Moore, Janelle 135
Moore, Supreme Court Justice Roy 148
Morgan County 91, 92
Morgan, John K. 43
Morris, Roy 239
Morton, Edna Jane Springfield 232
Morton, J. D. 214
Morton, Joseph W. 231
Morton, Sherman 232
Moses, Ansley 32
Motlow, Lem 20
Moultrie, Georgia 235
Mule Day 75, 76, 247
Murray, Smith 239
Muscle Shoals, Alabama 112
Muscle Shoals Canal Lock 112

N

National Register of Historical Places 98, 100, 103, 122, 178, 218, 226, 247
Neal, James F. 43
Neelley, Alvin Howard 164
Neelley, Judith Ann 164
Negro National League 69
Nelson, Willie 15
Newell, Carolyn 236
Nicely, Maury 239
Noccalula 105, 106, 107, 248
Norris, Clarence 153

O

Oconee, Georgia 207
Orange Grove Center 9, 13, 242
Orkin Exterminating Co. 170
Orme, former mining town of 110
Orne, Neil 76
Owen, Lew 59

P

Paige, Leroy "Satchel" 70
Painter, Denny 211
Pan, The 77
Paradise Garden 175, 177, 178, 248
Parker, Billy 239
Park, Jeff 214
Parton, Dolly 95, 170
Patten, General George 144
Patten, John A. 60
Patten, Zeboim Carter 59
Patterson, Albert 144
Patterson, Haywood 150
Patterson, John M. 141. 145, 178
Patterson, Tom 178
Paul, Dr. Rand 187
Paul, Dr. Ron 187
Payne, Captain John 102
Peacock, Robert 178
Peay, Governor Austin 21
Peerless Clipper 215, 248
Peerless Millers 214, 248
Peerless Woolen Mills 210, 211, 215, 248
Pehrson, Marnie L. 232
Penney, Sheriff E. 42
Persons, Gordon 145
Petros, Tennessee 77, 91, 94, 248
Phagan, Mary 197
Pharris, Jackson C. 182
Pharris, Janet 183
Phenix City 141, 144, 145, 146, 147, 248
Picasso, Pablo 175
Pickwick Landing Dam 111
Pine Breeze 80, 81, 82, 248
Piper, William 208
Pittsburgh, Georgia, 222
Plant Farm Museum 176
Pope, Dave 215
Pope, Joe 21

Pope, Jonathan 20
Pope, J. William 21
Pope, Lewis Shepherd 20
Presley, Elvis 35, 36, 176, 245, 248
Price, Delores 142
Price, Jo 80
Price, Victoria 150
Price, Vincent 168
Price, William Ralph "Shorty" 141, 142, 143
Pryor, Francis "Nappy" 49
Pryor, Richard 70
Pyle, Denver 168

R

Raft, George 168
Raney, Suzette 240
Ransom, John M. 229
Ray, James Earl 91
Reagan, President Ronald 133, 176
Reavely, "Doc" 214
redneck 192
Redwine, John G. 203
Reilly, John C. 180
Reisman, Dr. Edward 162
Rhea County 22, 45, 46, 47, 50, 63, 249
Rich, James M. 204
Ridley, Oscar 108
Riverton Lock. 112
Robbins, Mickey 13, 239
Robert B. French, Jr. 165
Roberts, Clyde 214
Roberts, Gene 42
Robertson, Dr. Lee 218
Robinson, Jackie 70
Rock Springs, Georgia 214
Roddy, Stephen 158
Rodgers, Jimmy 12
Rolfe, L. Monte 208
Rollins, O. Wayne 170
Rome, Georgia 23, 98, 164, 237

Roosevelt, Franklin Delano 111, 129
Rosecrans, General William 224
Rose, Larry 212
Rose, Pat 42
Rossville, Georgia 167, 210, 215
Rufolo, Jeff 12
Runge, Lorrie 32
Russel, Colonel Thomas 108
Russell Cave 101, 108, 109, 249
Ruth, Babe 24

S

Schalk, Marya 12
Schoolfield, Raulston 158, 173 242
Scott, Bobby 211
Scottsboro, Alabama 155
Scottsboro Boys 149, 150, 151, 152, 153, 155, 156, 157, 158
Self, Earl 237
Settles, Lee 214
Sewanee 27, 28, 85, 86, 87, 120, 121, 242, 249
Shaw, Barton C. 193
Shearer, John 240
Shelby, Richard 133
Sherman, General William T. 171
Sherrill, Billy 16
Short, Dave 85
Sies, Laurence Durwood 215
sin city 144
Skillet, The 77
Slage, James 91
Slaton, Governor John M. 198
Smith, Robert E. 167
Smitrovich, Bill 162
snake handling 66, 249
Sock Capital of the World. 103
Soddy Daisy, Tennessee 231
South Pittsburg, Tennessee 20, 48, 49, 50, 77, 79, 101, 108
Sparkman, John 133, 148

speed trap 48, 49, 249
Spring City, Tennessee 63
Steele, Orville (Pete) 236
Stevenson, Adlai E. 133
Stevenson, Alabama 99, 101, 133, 249
Stevenson, Vernon K. 100
Suck, The 77, 83, 84, 112, 249
Sullivan, Anne Mansfield 122, 123
Summerville, Georgia, 175
Summit, Pat 76
Swafford, Thomas K. 21
Swain, Francis M. 204

T

Talmadge, Governor Eugene 192, 234
Taylor, Robert L. 43
Taylor, Willis Lawrence 27
Tennessee Historical Society 240
Tennessee Valley Act (TVA) 83, 111, 112, 250
Test, Eddie 126
Thomas E. Knight 6, 155
Thomas, George 224
Thompson, Polly 125
Thornton, Harry 39
Townsend, John Murphy Clagett "Red" 172
Trail of Tears 77, 106, 249
Trammell, Patrick Lee 126, 127, 128
Trion, Georgia 175
Truman, Harry S. 135, 172, 182
Trump, Donald 185
tuberculosis (TB) 80
Tumbling Shoals 83
Turnage, Sylvia Dyer 205
Turner, James E. (Bookie) 42, 43, 44
Turner, Landis 38
Tuscumbia, Alabama 116, 122, 123, 132, 148
Tutwiler Hotel 114, 115, 135, 246, 250
Tutwiler, George Crawford Major 114

Twain, Mark 29, 30, 31

V

Valley Head, Alabama 175
Vass, Chris 13
Vick, J.T. 137

W

Wagner, Jack 51
Walker, Cas 35, 36, 95, 96
Walker, Clint 168
Walker County 168, 189, 190, 220, 221, 222, 223, 224, 225, 226, 227, 228, 229, 230, 231, 232, 237
Wallace, George Corley 136, 139, 141, 142, 148, 169
Wallace, Lurleen Burns 136
Wallace, Vice President Henry 135
Walsh, Ed 23
Wammack, Travis 117
Warrington, Pete 91
Washington, Booker T. 186
Washington, George 176
Waterloo, Alabama 111
Weaver, Buck 25
Weems, Charles 150
Wheat, Lamar 137
White, Gordon W. 42
Whiteside, James A. 100
Wickedest City in America 146
Wiehl, Fred F. 59
"Will" 27
Williams, Billy Dee 70
Williams, Eugene 159
Williams, Hank 135
Williams, Ron 82
Wilson, John 12
Wimpey, Johnny 204
Wine of Cardui 5, 8, 59, 60, 61, 62, 250
Wood, Norman 214
Woolens athletic team 210

Wool Hat Boys 192, 193, 250
Wooten, Junior 210
Wright, Moses 227
Wright, Orville and Wilbur 203 204,
    207, 250
Wright, Robert 227
Wynette, Tammy 170

Y

Young, Ambassador Andrew 186
Young, Loretta 194

www.ingramcontent.com/pod-product-compliance
Lightning Source LLC
Chambersburg PA
CBHW070524170426
43200CB00011B/2315